Composing Software

An Exploration of Functional Programming and Object Composition in JavaScript

Eric Elliott

Composing Software

An Exploration of Functional Programming and Object Composition in JavaScript

Eric Elliott

ISBN 9781661212568

Leanpub

This is a Leanpub book. Leanpub empowers authors and publishers with the Lean Publishing process. Lean Publishing is the act of publishing an in-progress ebook using lightweight tools and many iterations to get reader feedback, pivot until you have the right book and build traction once you do.

© 2017 - 2020 Eric Elliott

Contents

Thank You 1

Composing Software: An Introduction 3
    You Compose Software Every Day 4
    Conclusion 11

The Dao of Immutability (The Way of the Functional Programmer) 13
    Forward 13

The Rise and Fall and Rise of Functional Programming (Composable Software) 15
    The Rise of Functional Programming 15
    The Fall of Functional Programming 18
    The Rise of Functional Programming 18
    Functional Programming Has Always Been Alive and Well 19

Why Learn Functional Programming in JavaScript? 21

Pure Functions 29
    What is a Function? 29
    Mapping 29
    Pure Functions 30
    The Trouble with Shared State 31
    Same Input, Same Output 32
    No Side Effects 33
    Conclusion 36

What is Functional Programming? 37
    Pure Functions 38
    Function Composition 38
    Shared State 38
    Immutability 41
    Side Effects 42
    Reusability Through Higher Order Functions 42
    Containers, Functors, Lists, and Streams 43
    Declarative vs Imperative 44

CONTENTS

    Conclusion 45

A Functional Programmer's Introduction to JavaScript 47
    Expressions and Values 47
    Types 48
    Destructuring 49
    Comparisons and Ternaries 50
    Functions 51
    Currying 55
    Function Composition 57
    Arrays 58
    Method Chaining 58
    Conclusion 59

Higher Order Functions 61

Curry and Function Composition 65
    What is a curried function? 65
    What is a partial application? 66
    What's the Difference? 66
    What is point-free style? 66
    Why do we curry? 67
    Trace 69
    Curry and Function Composition, Together 70
    Conclusion 75

Abstraction & Composition 77
    Abstraction is simplification. 78
    Abstraction in Software 78
    Abstraction through composition 79
    How to Do More with Less Code 80
    Conclusion 81
    Reduce 81
    Reduce is Versatile 82
    Conclusion 86

Functors & Categories 87
    Why Functors? 88
    Functor Laws 92
    Category Theory 93
    Build Your Own Functor 95
    Curried Map 96
    Conclusion 97

Monads 99
You're probably already using monads. 101
What Monads are Made of 106
Building a Kleisli Composition Function 109
The Monad Laws 112
Conclusion 116

The Forgotten History of OOP 117
The Big Idea 118
The Essence of OOP 120
What OOP Doesn't Mean 121
What is an object? 123
We've lost the plot. 124

Object Composition 127
What is Object Composition? 128
Three Different Forms of Object Composition 129
Notes on Code Examples 129
Aggregation 130
Concatenation 132
Delegation 133
Conclusion 135

Factory Functions 137
Literals for One, Factories for Many 138
Returning Objects 139
Destructuring 139
Computed Property Keys 140
Default Parameters 141
Type Inference 142
Factory Functions for Mixin Composition 144
Conclusion 146

Functional Mixins 149
Motivation 149
What are mixins? 150
What is functional inheritance? 151
What is a functional mixin? 152
Composing Functional Mixins 153
When to Use Functional Mixins 154
Caveats 154
Conclusion 159

Why Composition is Harder with Classes 161

    The Delegate Prototype 161
    The `.constructor` Property 163
    Class to Factory is a Breaking Change 166

Composable Custom Data Types 173
    You can do this with any data type 176
    Composable Currency 176

Lenses 179
    Why Lenses? 180
    Background 180
    Lens Laws 181
    Composing Lenses 183

Transducers 187
    Why Transducers? 188
    Background and Etymology 190
    A Musical Analogy for Transducers 192
    Transducers compose top-to-bottom. 198
    Transducer Rules 198
    Transducing 200
    The Transducer Protocol 202
    Conclusion 203

Elements of JavaScript Style 205
    1. Make the function the unit of composition. One job for each function. 205
    2. Omit needless code. 206
    3. Use active voice. 210
    4. Avoid a succession of loose statements. 212
    5. Keep related code together. 213
    6. Put statements and expressions in positive form. 214
    7. Use parallel code for parallel concepts. 215
    Conclusion: Code should be simple, not simplistic. 216

Mocking is a Code Smell 219
    TDD should lead to better design. 219
    What is a code smell? 220
    What is a mock? 220
    What is a unit test? 221
    What is test coverage? 221
    What is tight coupling? 222
    What causes tight coupling? 223
    What does composition have to do with mocking? 223
    How do we remove coupling? 226

"Code smells" are warning signs, not laws. Mocks are not evil. 234

Thank You

To my editor, JS Cheerleader, who made this book much better in too many ways to list. If you find the text readable, it is because she carefully pored over every page and offered insightful feedback and encouragement every step of the way. Without her help, you would not be reading this book right now.

To the blog readers, whose support and enthusiasm helped us turn a little blog post series into a phenomenon that attracted millions of readers and provided the momentum we needed to turn it into a book.

To the legends of computer science who paved the way.

> "If I have seen further it is by standing on the shoulders of Giants." ~ Sir Isaac Newton

Composing Software: An Introduction

Composition: "The act of combining parts or elements to form a whole." ~ Dictionary.com

In my first high school programming class, I was instructed that software development is "the act of breaking a complex problem down into smaller problems, and composing simple solutions to form a complete solution to the complex problem."

One of my biggest regrets in life is that I failed to understand the significance of that lesson early on. I learned the essence of software design far too late in life.

I have interviewed hundreds of developers. What I've learned from those sessions is that I'm not alone. Very few working software developers have a good grasp on the essence of software development. They aren't aware of the most important tools we have at our disposal, or how to put them to good use. 100% have struggled to answer one or both of the most important questions in the field of software development:

- What is function composition?
- What is object composition?

The problem is that you can't avoid composition just because you're not aware of it. You still do it – but you do it badly. You write code with more bugs, and make it harder for other developers to understand. This is a big problem. The effects are very costly. We spend more time maintaining software than we do creating it from scratch, and our bugs impact billions of people all over the world.

The entire world runs on software today. Every new car is a mini super-computer on wheels, and problems with software design cause real accidents and cost real human lives. In 2013, a jury found Toyota's software development team guilty of "reckless disregard"[1] after an accident investigation revealed spaghetti code with 10,000 global variables.

Hackers and governments stockpile bugs[2] in order to spy on people, steal credit cards, harness computing resources to launch Distributed Denial of Service (DDoS) attacks, crack passwords, and even manipulate elections[3].

We must do better.

---

[1] http://www.safetyresearch.net/blog/articles/toyota-unintended-acceleration-and-big-bowl-%E2%80%9Cspaghetti%E2%80%9D-code
[2] https://www.technologyreview.com/s/607875/should-the-government-keep-stockpiling-software-bugs/
[3] https://www.technologyreview.com/s/604138/the-fbi-shut-down-a-huge-botnet-but-there-are-plenty-more-left/

You Compose Software Every Day

If you're a software developer, you compose functions and data structures every day, whether you know it or not. You can do it consciously (and better), or you can do it accidentally, with duct-tape and crazy glue.

The process of software development is breaking down large problems into smaller problems, building components that solve those smaller problems, then composing those components together to form a complete application.

Composing Functions

Function composition is the process of applying a function to the output of another function. In algebra, given two functions, f and g, $(f \circ g)(x) = f(g(x))$. The circle is the composition operator. It's commonly pronounced "composed with" or "after". You can say that out-loud as "f *composed with* g equals f of g of x", or "f *after* g equals f of g of x". We say f *after* g because g is evaluated first, then its output is passed as an argument to f.

Every time you write code like this, you're composing functions:

```javascript
const g = n => n + 1;
const f = n => n * 2;

const doStuff = x => {
  const afterG = g(x);
  const afterF = f(afterG);
  return afterF;
};

doStuff(20); // 42
```

Every time you write a promise chain, you're composing functions:

```javascript
const g = n => n + 1;
const f = n => n * 2;

const wait = time => new Promise(
  (resolve, reject) => setTimeout(
    resolve,
    time
  )
);

```

```
11  wait(300)
12    .then(() => 20)
13    .then(g)
14    .then(f)
15    .then(value => console.log(value)) // 42
16  ;
```

Likewise, every time you chain array method calls, lodash methods, observables (RxJS, etc...) you're composing functions. If you're chaining, you're composing. If you're passing return values into other functions, you're composing. If you call two methods in a sequence, you're composing using this as input data.

> If you're chaining, you're composing.

When you compose functions intentionally, you'll do it better.

Composing functions intentionally, we can improve our doStuff() function to a simple one-liner:

```
1  const g = n => n + 1;
2  const f = n => n * 2;
3
4  const doStuffBetter = x => f(g(x));
5
6  doStuffBetter(20); // 42
```

A common objection to this form is that it's harder to debug. For example, how would we write this using function composition?

```
1  const doStuff = x => {
2    const afterG = g(x);
3    console.log(`after g: ${ afterG }`);
4    const afterF = f(afterG);
5    console.log(`after f: ${ afterF }`);
6    return afterF;
7  };
8
9  doStuff(20); // =>
10 /*
11 "after g: 21"
12 "after f: 42"
13 */
```

First, let's abstract that "after f", "after g" logging into a little utility called trace():

```javascript
const trace = label => value => {
  console.log(`${ label }: ${ value }`);
  return value;
};
```

Now we can use it like this:

```javascript
const doStuff = x => {
  const afterG = g(x);
  trace('after g')(afterG);
  const afterF = f(afterG);
  trace('after f')(afterF);
  return afterF;
};

doStuff(20); // =>
/*
"after g: 21"
"after f: 42"
*/
```

Popular functional programming libraries like Lodash and Ramda include utilities to make function composition easier. You can rewrite the above function like this:

```javascript
import pipe from 'lodash/fp/flow';

const doStuffBetter = pipe(
  g,
  trace('after g'),
  f,
  trace('after f')
);

doStuffBetter(20); // =>
/*
"after g: 21"
"after f: 42"
*/
```

If you want to try this code without importing something, you can define pipe like this:

```
1  // pipe(...fns: [...Function]) => x => y
2  const pipe = (...fns) => x => fns.reduce((y, f) => f(y), x);
```

Don't worry if you're not following how that works, yet. Later on we'll explore function composition in a lot more detail. In fact, it's so essential, you'll see it defined and demonstrated many times throughout this text. The point is to help you become so familiar with it that its definition and usage becomes automatic. Be one with the composition.

`pipe()` creates a pipeline of functions, passing the output of one function to the input of another. When you use `pipe()` (and its twin, `compose()`) You don't need intermediary variables. Writing functions without mention of the arguments is called "point-free style". To do it, you'll call a function that returns the new function, rather than declaring the function explicitly. That means you won't need the `function` keyword or the arrow syntax (=>).

Point-free style can be taken too far, but a little bit here and there is great because those intermediary variables add unnecessary complexity to your functions.

There are several benefits to reduced complexity:

Working Memory

The average human has only a few shared resources for discrete quanta in working memory[4], and each variable potentially consumes one of those quanta. As you add more variables, our ability to accurately recall the meaning of each variable is diminished. Working memory models typically involve 4-7 discrete quanta. Above those numbers, error rates dramatically increase.

Using the pipe form, we eliminated 3 variables – freeing up almost half of our available working memory for other things. That reduces our cognitive load significantly. Software developers tend to be better at chunking data into working memory than the average person, but not so much more as to weaken the importance of conservation.

Signal to Noise Ratio

Concise code also improves the signal-to-noise ratio of your code. It's like listening to a radio – when the radio is not tuned properly to the station, you get a lot of interfering noise, and it's harder to hear the music. When you tune it to the correct station, the noise goes away, and you get a stronger musical signal.

Code is the same way. More concise code expression leads to enhanced comprehension. Some code gives us useful information, and some code just takes up space. If you can reduce the amount of code you use without reducing the meaning that gets transmitted, you'll make the code easier to parse and understand for other people who need to read it.

---

[4]http://www.nature.com/neuro/journal/v17/n3/fig_tab/nn.3655_F2.html

Surface Area for Bugs

Take a look at the before and after functions. It looks like the function went on a diet and lost a ton of weight. That's important because extra code means extra surface area for bugs to hide in, which means more bugs will hide in it. *Less code = less surface area for bugs = fewer bugs.*

Composing Objects

> "Favor object composition over class inheritance" the Gang of Four, "Design Patterns: Elements of Reusable Object Oriented Software"[5]

> "In computer science, **a composite data type** or compound data type is any data type which can be constructed in a program using the programming language's primitive data types and other composite types. [...] The act of constructing a composite type is known as composition." ~ Wikipedia

These are primitives:

```
const firstName = 'Claude';
const lastName = 'Debussy';
```

And this is a composite:

```
const fullName = {
  firstName,
  lastName
};
```

Likewise, all Arrays, Sets, Maps, WeakMaps, TypedArrays, etc... are composite datatypes. Any time you build any non-primitive data structure, **you're performing some kind of object composition**.

Note that the Gang of Four defines a pattern called the *composite pattern* which is a specific type of recursive object composition which allows you to treat individual components and aggregated composites identically. Some developers get confused, thinking that the composite pattern is *the only form of object composition*. Don't get confused. There are many different kinds of object composition.

The Gang of Four continues, "you'll see object composition applied again and again in design patterns", and then they catalog three kinds of object compositional relationships, including **delegation** (when an object delegates property access to another object, as used in the state, strategy, and visitor patterns), **acquaintance** (when an object knows about another object by reference, usually passed as a parameter: a uses-a relationship, e.g., a network request handler might be passed

---

[5]https://www.amazon.com/Design-Patterns-Elements-Reusable-Object-Oriented/dp/0201633612/ref=as_li_ss_tl?ie=UTF8&qid=1494993475&sr=8-1&keywords=design+patterns&linkCode=ll1&tag=eejs-20&linkId=6c553f16325f3939e5abadd4ee04e8b4

a reference to a logger to log the request—the request handler *uses* a logger), and **aggregation** (when child objects form part of a parent object: a has-a relationship, e.g., DOM children are component elements in a DOM node—A DOM node *has* children).

Class inheritance can be used to construct composite objects, but it's a restrictive and brittle way to do it. When the Gang of Four says "favor object composition over class inheritance", they're advising you to use flexible approaches to composite object building, rather than the rigid, tightly-coupled approach of class inheritance. They're encouraging you to favor has-a and uses-a relationships over is-a relationships.

Rather than refer to specific design patterns, we'll use a more general definition of object composition from "Categorical Methods in Computer Science: With Aspects from Topology"[6] (1989):

> "Composite objects are formed by putting objects together such that each of the latter is 'part of' the former."

Another good reference is "Reliable Software Through Composite Design", Glenford J Myers, 1975. Both books are long out of print, but you can still find sellers on Amazon or eBay if you'd like to explore the subject of object composition in more technical depth and historical context.

Class inheritance is just one kind of composite object construction. All classes produce composite objects, but not all composite objects are produced by classes or class inheritance. "Favor object composition over class inheritance" means that you should form composite objects from small component parts, rather than inheriting all properties from an ancestor in a class hierarchy. The latter causes a large variety of well-known problems in object oriented design:

- **The tight coupling problem**: Because child classes are dependent on the implementation of the parent class, class inheritance is the tightest coupling available in object oriented design.
- **The fragile base class problem**: Due to tight coupling, changes to the base class can potentially break a large number of descendant classes – potentially in code managed by third parties. The author could break code they're not aware of.
- **The inflexible hierarchy problem**: With single ancestor taxonomies, given enough time and evolution, all class taxonomies are eventually wrong for new use-cases.
- **The duplication by necessity problem**: Due to inflexible hierarchies, new use cases are often implemented by duplication, rather than extension, leading to similar classes which are unexpectedly divergent. Once duplication sets in, it's not obvious which class new classes should descend from, or why.
- **The gorilla/banana problem**: "…the problem with object-oriented languages is they've got all this implicit environment that they carry around with them. You wanted a banana but what you got was a gorilla holding the banana and the entire jungle." ~ Joe Armstrong, "Coders at Work"[7]

---

[6]https://www.amazon.com/Categorical-Methods-Computer-Science-Topology/dp/0387517227/ref=as_li_ss_tl?ie=UTF8&qid=1495077930&sr=8-3&keywords=Categorical+Methods+in+Computer+Science:+With+Aspects+from+Topology&linkCode=ll1&tag=eejs-20&linkId=095afed5272832b74357f63b41410cb7

[7]http://www.amazon.com/gp/product/1430219483?ie=UTF8&camp=213733&creative=393185&creativeASIN=1430219483&linkCode=shr&tag=eejs-20&linkId=3MNWRRZU3C4Q4BDN

The most common form of object composition in JavaScript is known as **object concatenation** (aka, **concatenative inheritance**: informally, "mixin composition"). It works like ice-cream. You start with an object (like vanilla ice-cream), and then mix in the features you want. Add some nuts, caramel, chocolate swirl, and you wind up with nutty caramel chocolate swirl ice cream.

Building composites with class inheritance:

```javascript
class Foo {
  constructor () {
    this.a = 'a'
  }
}

class Bar extends Foo {
  constructor (options) {
    super(options);
    this.b = 'b'
  }
}

const myBar = new Bar(); // {a: 'a', b: 'b'}
```

Building composites with mixin composition:

```javascript
const a = {
  a: 'a'
};

const b = {
  b: 'b'
};

const c = {...a, ...b}; // {a: 'a', b: 'b'}
```

We'll explore other styles of object composition in more depth later. For now, your understanding should be:

1. There's more than one way to do it.
2. Some ways are better than others.
3. You want to select the simplest, most flexible solution for the task at hand.

Conclusion

This isn't about functional programming (FP) vs object-oriented programming (OOP), or one language vs another. Components can take the form of functions, data structures, classes, etc... Different programming languages tend to afford different atomic elements for components. Java affords objects, Haskell affords functions, etc... But no matter what language and what paradigm you favor, you can't get away from composing functions and data structures. In the end, that's what it all boils down to.

We'll talk a lot about functional programming, because functions are the simplest things to compose in JavaScript, and the functional programming community has invested a lot of time and effort formalizing function composition techniques.

What we won't do is say that functional programming is better than object-oriented programming, or that you must choose one over the other. OOP vs FP is a false dichotomy. Every real Javascript application I've seen in recent years mixes FP and OOP extensively.

We'll use object composition to produce datatypes for functional programming, and functional programming to produce objects for OOP.

No matter how you write software, you should compose it well.

> The essence of software development is composition.

A software developer who doesn't understand composition is like a home builder who doesn't know about bolts or nails. Building software without awareness of composition is like a home builder putting walls together with duct tape and crazy glue.

It's time to simplify, and the best way to simplify is to get to the essence. The trouble is, almost nobody in the industry has a good handle on the essentials. We as an industry have failed you, the software developer. It's our responsibility as an industry to train developers better. We must improve. We need to take responsibility. Everything runs on software today, from the economy to medical equipment. There is literally no corner of human life on this planet that is not impacted by the quality of our software. We need to know what we're doing.

It's time to learn how to compose software.

The Dao of Immutability (The Way of the Functional Programmer)

Functional programming is a foundational pillar of JavaScript, and immutability is a foundational pillar of functional programming. You can't fully understand functional programming without first understanding immutability. This story may help.

Forward

I was wandering the archives of an old library, and found a dark tunnel that led to the chamber of computation. There I found a scroll that seemed to have fallen on the floor, forgotten.

The scroll was encased in a dusty steel tube and labeled: "From the archives of The Church of Lambda."

It was wrapped in a thin sheet of paper that read:

A master programmer and his apprentice sat in Turing meditation, contemplating the Lambda. The apprentice looked at the master and asked, "Master, you tell me to simplify, but programs are complex. Frameworks ease the work of creation by removing hard choices. Which is better, a class or a framework?" The master programmer looked at his apprentice and asked, "did you not read the teachings of wise master Carmack?", quoting...

> "Sometimes, the elegant implementation is just a function. Not a method. Not a class. Not a framework. Just a function."

"But master," the apprentice started —â€Šbut the master interrupted, asking:

"Is it not true that the word for 'not functional' is 'dysfunctional'?"

And then the apprentice understood.

On the back of the sheet was an index that seemed to refer to many books in the chamber of computation. I peeked inside the books, but they were filled with big words I did not understand, so I put them back and continued to read the scroll. I noticed that the margins of the index were filled with short commentary, which I will reproduce here, faithfully, along with the writing from the scroll:

> **Immutability**: The true constant is change. Mutation hides change. Hidden change manifests chaos. Therefore, the wise embrace history.

If you have a dollar, and I give you another dollar, it does not change the fact that a moment ago you only had one dollar, and now you have two. Mutation attempts to erase history, but history cannot be truly erased. When the past is not preserved, it will come back to haunt you, manifesting as bugs in the program.

> **Separation**: Logic is thought. Effects are action. Therefore the wise think before acting, and act only when the thinking is done.

If you try to perform effects and logic at the same time, you may create hidden side effects which cause bugs in the logic. Keep functions small. Do one thing at a time, and do it well.

> **Composition**: All things in nature work in harmony. A tree cannot grow without water. A bird cannot fly without air. Therefore the wise mix ingredients together to make their soup taste better.

Plan for composition. Write functions whose outputs will naturally work as inputs to many other functions. Keep function signatures as simple as possible. Conservation: Time is precious, and effort takes time. Therefore the wise reuse their tools as much as they can. The foolish create special tools for each new creation.

Type-specific functions can't be reused for data of a different type. Wise programmers lift functions to work on many data types, or wrap data to make it look like what the function is expecting. Lists and items make great universal abstractions.

> **Flow**: still waters are unsafe to drink. Food left alone will rot. The wise prosper because they let things flow.

[Editor's note: The only illustration on the scroll was a row of different-looking ducks floating down a stream just above this verse. I have not reproduced the illustration because I don't believe I could do it justice. Curiously, it was captioned:]

> A list expressed over time is a stream.

[The corresponding note read:]

Shared objects and data fixtures can cause functions to interfere with each other. Threads competing for the same resources can trip each other up. A program can be reasoned about and outcomes predicted only when data flows freely through pure functions.

[Editor's note: The scroll ended with this final verse, which had no commentary:]

> **Wisdom**: The wise programmer understands the way before walking the path. Therefore the wise programmer is functional, while the unwise get lost in *the jungle*.

The Rise and Fall and Rise of Functional Programming (Composable Software)

When I was about 6 years old, I spent a lot of time playing computer games with my best friend. His family had a room full of computers. To me, they were irresistible. Magic. I spent many hours exploring all the games. One day I asked my friend, "how do we make a game?"

He didn't know, so we asked his dad, who reached up on a high shelf and pulled down a book of games written in basic. So began my journey with programming. By the time public school got around to teaching algebra, I already knew the topic well, because programming is basically algebra. It can be, anyway.

The Rise of Functional Programming

In the beginning of computer science, before most of computer science was actually done on computers, there lived two great mathematicians: Alonzo Church, and Alan Turing. They produced two different, but equivalent universal models of computation. Both models could compute any function computable by a Turing machine, meaning, given input n, there is a Turing machine that eventually halts and returns f(n).

Alonzo Church invented lambda calculus. **Lambda calculus** is a universal model of computation based on **function application**. Alan Turing is known for the Turing machine. A **Turing machine** is a universal model of computation that defines a theoretical device that manipulates symbols on a strip of tape. As Turing put it:

> "A function is effectively calculable if its values can be found by some purely mechanical process." ~ A.M Turing, "Systems of Logic Based on Ordinals[8]"

The Church Turing Thesis shows that lambda calculus and the Turing machine are equivalent.

In lambda calculus, functions are king. Everything is a function, including numbers. Thinking of functions as the atomic building blocks (the legos from which we construct our creations) is a remarkably expressive and eloquent way to compose software. In this text, we're going to discuss the importance of function composition in software design.

There are three important points that make lambda calculus special:

---

[8]https://webspace.princeton.edu/users/jedwards/Turing%20Centennial%202012/Mudd%20Archive%20files/12285_AC100_Turing_1938.pdf

1. Functions are always anonymous. In JavaScript, the right side of `const sum = (x, y) => x + y` is the *anonymous* function expression `(x, y) => x + y`.
2. Functions in lambda calculus are *always unary*, meaning they only accept a single parameter. If you need more than one parameter, the function will take one input and return a new function that takes the next, and so on until all the parameters have been collected and the function application can complete. The n-ary function `(x, y) => x + y` can be expressed as a unary function like: `x => y => x + y`. This transformation from an n-ary function to a series of unary functions is known as currying.
3. Functions are first-class, meaning that functions can be used as inputs to other functions, and functions can return functions.

Together, these features form a simple, yet expressive vocabulary for composing software using functions as the primary building block. In JavaScript, anonymous functions and curried functions are optional features. While JavaScript supports important features of lambda calculus, it does not enforce them.

The classic function composition takes the output from one function and uses it as the input for another function. For example, the composition `f . g` can be written as:

```
const compose = (f, g) => x => f(g(x));
```

Here's how you'd use it:

```
const compose = (f, g) => x => f(g(x));

const double = n => n * 2;
const inc = n => n + 1;

const transform = compose(double, inc);

transform(3); // 8
```

The `compose()` function takes the `double` function as the first argument, the `inc` function as the second, and returns a function that combines the two. Inside the `compose()` function when `transform()` gets invoked, f is `double()`, g is `inc()`, and x is 3:

1. x evaluates to 3 and gets passed into `inc()`.
2. `inc(3)` evaluates to 4.
3. `double(4)` evaluates to 8.
4. 8 gets returned from the composed function.

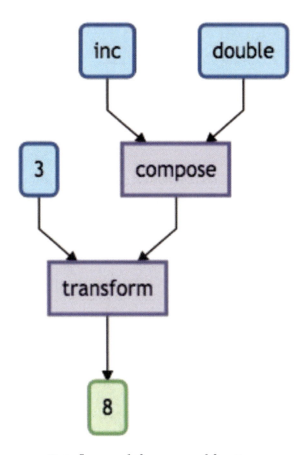

Data flow graph for composed functions

Lambda calculus was hugely influential on software design, and prior to about 1980, many very influential icons of computer science were building software using function composition. Lisp was created in 1958, and was heavily influenced by lambda calculus. Today, Lisp is the second-oldest language that's still in popular use.

I was introduced to it through AutoLISP: the scripting language used in the most popular Computer Aided Design (CAD) software: AutoCAD. AutoCAD is so popular, virtually every other CAD application supports AutoLISP so that they can be compatible. Lisp is also a popular teaching language in computer science curriculum for three reasons:

1. Its simplicity makes it easy to learn the basic syntax and semantics of Lisp in about a day.
2. Lisp is all about function composition, and function composition is an elegant way to structure applications.
3. My favorite computer science text uses Lisp: Structure and Interpretation of Computer Programs[9].

---

[9]https://www.amazon.com/Structure-Interpretation-Computer-Programs-Engineering/dp/0262510871/ref=as_li_ss_tl?ie=UTF8&linkCode=ll1&tag=eejs-20&linkId=4896ed63eee8657b6379c2acd99dd3f3

The Fall of Functional Programming

Somewhere between 1970 and 1980, the way that software was composed drifted away from simple algebraic math, and became a list of linear instructions for the computer to follow in languages like K&R C (1978) and the tiny BASIC interpretters that shipped with the early home computers of the 1970s and early 1980s.

In 1972, Alan Kay's Smalltalk was formalized, and the idea of objects as the atomic unit of composition took hold. Smalltalk's great idea about component encapsulation and message passing got distorted in the 80s and 90s by C++ and Java into a horrible idea about inheritance hierarchies and **is-a** relationships for feature reuse.

Even though Smalltalk was a functional OOP language, when C++ and Java took over mindshare, functional programming was relegated to the sidelines and academia: The blissful obsession of the geekiest of programming geeks, professors in their ivy towers, and some lucky students who escaped the Java force-feeding obsession of the 1990s - 2010.

For most of us, creating software was a bit of a nightmare for 30 years. Dark times. ;)

> **Note**: I learned to code with Basic, Pascal, C++, and Java. I used AutoLisp to manipulate 3D graphics. Only AutoLisp is functional. For the first several years of my programming career, I didn't realize functional programming was a practical option outside the realm of vector graphics programming.

The Rise of Functional Programming

Around 2010, something great began to happen: JavaScript exploded. Before about 2006, JavaScript was widely considered a toy language used to make cute animations happen in web browsers, but it had some powerful features hidden in it. Namely, the most important features of lambda calculus. People started whispering in the shadows about this cool thing called "functional programming".

By 2015, the idea of functional programming was popular again. To make it simpler, the JavaScript specification got its first major upgrade of the decade and added the arrow function, which made it easier to create and read functions, currying, and lambda expressions.

Arrow functions were like rocket fuel for the functional programming explosion in JavaScript. Today it's rare to see a large application which doesn't use a lot of functional programming techniques.

Composition is a simple, elegant, and expressive way to clearly model the behavior of software. The process of composing small, deterministic functions to create larger software components and functionality produces software that is easier to organize, understand, debug, extend, test, and maintain.

Functional Programming Has Always Been Alive and Well

In spite of this tongue-in-cheek stab at popular languages, functional programming has always been alive and well. Lisp and Smalltalk were among C's biggest competitors in the industrial landscape of the 1980s and 1990s. Smalltalk was a popular enterprise software solution at fortune 500 companies including **JPMorgan Chase**[10], and Lisp was used at **NASA JPL** to program Mars rovers[11].

Lisp was and is still used at **Stanford Research Institute (SRI)** for artificial intelligence and bioinformatics research. (SRI is where the technology behind Apple's SIRI virtual assistant was developed). **YCombinator,** one of the most influential venture capital firms in Silicon Valley was cofounded by Paul Graham, who is an influencer in the Lisp community. The popular tech news site, **Hacker News**[12] was written in Ark, a dialect of Lisp.

Clojure, a Lisp dialect, was created by Rich Hickey in 2007 and quickly gained popularity and use at major tech companies including **Amazon**, **Apple**, and **Facebook**.

Erlang is a popular functional programming language developed at **Ericsson** for use in telephone exchanges. It's still used in mobile networks by **T-Mobile**. **Amazon** uses Erlang for cloud technologies including SimpleDB and Elastic Compute Cloud (EC2).

All that said, as the standard language of the web, JavaScript is the most popular programming language in the world, and JavaScript has exposed an unprecedented number of developers to the functional programming paradigm.

---

[10]http://www.cincomsmalltalk.com/main/successes/financial-services/jpmorgan/
[11]http://www.flownet.com/gat/jpl-lisp.html
[12]https://news.ycombinator.com/

Why Learn Functional Programming in JavaScript?

Forget whatever you think you know about JavaScript, and approach this material with a beginner's mind. To help you do that, we're going to review the JavaScript basics from the ground up, as if you've never seen JavaScript before. If you're a beginner, you're in luck. Finally something exploring ES6 and functional programming from scratch! Hopefully all the new concepts are explained along the way – but don't count on too much pampering.

If you're a seasoned developer already familiar with JavaScript, or a pure functional language, maybe you're thinking that JavaScript is a funny choice for an exploration of functional programming. Set those thoughts aside, and try to approach the material with an open mind. You may find that there is another level to JavaScript programming. One you never knew existed.

Since this text is called "Composing Software", and functional programming is the obvious way to compose software (using function composition, higher order functions, etc...), you may be wondering why I'm not talking about Haskell, ClojureScript, or Elm, instead of JavaScript.

JavaScript has the most important features needed for functional programming:

1. **First class functions**: The ability to use functions as data values: pass functions as arguments, return functions, and assign functions to variables and object properties. This property allows for higher order functions, which enable partial application, currying, and composition.
2. **Anonymous functions and concise lambda syntax**: `x => x * 2` is a valid function expression in JavaScript. Concise lambdas make it easier to work with higher-order functions.
3. **Closures**: A closure is the bundling of a function with its lexical environment. Closures are created at function creation time. When a function is defined inside another function, it has access to the variable bindings in the outer function, even after the outer function exits. Closures are how partial applications get their fixed arguments. A **fixed** argument is an argument bound in the closure scope of a returned function. In `add2(1)(2)`, `1` is a fixed argument in the function returned by `add2(1)`.

What JavaScript is Missing

JavaScript is a multi-paradigm language, meaning that it supports programming in many different styles. Other styles supported by JavaScript include procedural (imperative) programming (like C), where functions represent a subroutine of instructions that can be called repeatedly for reuse and organization, object-oriented programming, where objects – not functions – are the primary building blocks, and of course, functional programming. The disadvantage of a multi-paradigm language is that imperative and object-oriented programming tend to imply that almost everything needs to be mutable.

Mutation is a change to data structure that happens in-place. For example:

```
1  const foo = {
2    bar: 'baz'
3  };
4
5  foo.bar = 'qux'; // mutation
```

Objects usually need to be mutable so that their properties can be updated by methods. In imperative programming, most data structures are mutable to enable efficient in-place manipulation of objects and arrays.

Here are some features that some functional languages have, that JavaScript does not have:

1. **Purity**: In some FP languages, purity is enforced by the language. Expressions with side-effects are not allowed.
2. **Immutability**: Some FP languages disable mutations. Instead of mutating an existing data structure, such as an array or object, expressions evaluate to new data structures. This may sound inefficient, but most functional languages use trie data structures under the hood, which feature structural sharing: meaning that the old object and new object share references to the data that is the same.
3. **Recursion**: Recursion is the ability for a function to reference itself for the purpose of iteration. In many FP languages, recursion is the only way to iterate. There are no loop statements like `for`, `while`, or `do` loops.

Purity: In JavaScript, purity must be achieved by convention. If you're not building most of your application by composing pure functions, you're not programming using the functional style. It's unfortunately easy in JavaScript to get off track by accidentally creating and using impure functions.

Immutability: In pure functional languages, immutability is often enforced. JavaScript lacks efficient, immutable trie-based data structures used by most functional languages, but there are libraries that help, including Immutable.js[13] and Mori[14]. I'm hoping that future versions of the ECMAScript spec will embrace immutable data structures. There are signs that offer hope, like the addition of the `const` keyword in ES6. A name binding defined with `const` can't be reassigned to refer to a different value. It's important to understand that `const` does not represent an immutable *value*.

A `const` object can't be reassigned to refer to a completely different object, but the object it refers to *can have its properties mutated*. JavaScript also has the ability to `freeze()` objects, but those objects are only frozen at the root level, meaning that a nested object can still have properties of

---

[13]https://facebook.github.io/immutable-js/
[14]https://github.com/swannodette/mori

its properties mutated. In other words, there's still a long road ahead before we see true composite immutables in the JavaScript specification.

Recursion: JavaScript technically supports recursion, but most functional languages have a feature called proper tail calls. **Proper tail calls** are a language feature which allows recursive functions to reuse stack frames for recursive calls.

Without proper tail calls, a call stack can grow without bounds and cause a stack overflow. JavaScript technically got proper tail calls in the ES6 specification. Unfortunately, only one of the major browser engines enabled it as a default feature, and the optimization was partially implemented and then subsequently removed from Babel (the most popular standard JavaScript compiler, used to compile ES6 to ES5 for use in older browsers).

Bottom line: It still isn't safe to use recursion for large iterations — even if you're careful to call the function in the tail position.

What JavaScript Has that Pure Functional Languages Lack

A purist will tell you that JavaScript's mutability is its major disadvantage, which is sometimes true. However, side effects and mutation are sometimes beneficial. In fact, it's impossible to create most useful modern applications without effects. Pure functional languages like Haskell use effects, but camouflage them from pure functions using boxes called monads, allowing the program to remain pure even though the effects represented by the monads are impure.

The trouble with monads is that, even though their use is quite simple, explaining what a monad is to somebody unfamiliar with lots of examples is a bit like explaining what the color "blue" looks like to a blind person. In it's most basic form, a monad is simply a data type that maps and flattens in one operation (covered in much more depth later). But to get an intuition for how they're used and the flexibility they give us, you really just need to jump in and start using them. If you're using promises or the new `Array.prototype.flatMap()` method, you're already on your way.

But learning them for the first time can be seriously intimidating, and the idiomatic literature on the topic isn't helping:

> "A monad is a monoid in the category of endofunctors, what's the problem?" ~ James Iry, fictionally quoting Philip Wadler, paraphrasing a real quote by Saunders Mac Lane. "A Brief, Incomplete, and Mostly Wrong History of Programming Languages"[15]

Typically, parody exaggerates things to make a funny point funnier. In the quote above, the explanation of monads is actually *simplified* from the original quote, which goes like this:

> "A monad in X is just a monoid in the category of endofunctors of X, with product Ã– replaced by composition of endofunctors and unit set by the identity endofunctor." ~ Saunders Mac Lane. "Categories for the Working Mathematician"[16]

---

[15] http://james-iry.blogspot.com/2009/05/brief-incomplete-and-mostly-wrong.html
[16] https://www.amazon.com/Categories-Working-Mathematician-Graduate-Mathematics/dp/0387984038//ref=as_li_ss_tl?ie=UTF8&linkCode=ll1&tag=eejs-20&linkId=de6f23899da4b5892f562413173be4f0

Even so, in my opinion, fear of monads is weak reasoning. The best way to learn monads is not to read a bunch of books and blog posts on the subject, but to jump in and start using them. As with most things in functional programming, the impenetrable academic vocabulary is much harder to understand than the concepts. Trust me, you don't have to understand Saunders Mac Lane to understand functional programming.

While it may not be absolutely ideal for every programmming style, JavaScript is unapologetically a general-purpose language designed to be usable by various people with various programming styles and backgrounds.

According to Brendan Eich[17], this was intentional from the beginning. Netscape had to support two kinds of programmers:

> "...the component authors, who wrote in C++ or (we hoped) Java; and the 'scripters', amateur or pro, who would write code directly embedded in HTML."

Originally, the intent was that Netscape would support two different languages, and the scripting language would probably resemble Scheme (a dialect of Lisp). Again, Brendan Eich:

> "I was recruited to Netscape with the promise of 'doing Scheme' in the browser."

JavaScript had to be a new language:

> "The *diktat* from upper engineering management was that the language must 'look like Java'. That ruled out Perl, Python, and Tcl, along with Scheme."

So, the ideas in Brendan Eich's head from the beginning were:

1. Scheme in the browser.
2. Look like Java.

It ended up being even more of a mish-mash:

> "I'm not proud, but I'm happy that I chose Scheme-ish first-class functions and Self-ish (albeit singular) prototypes as the main ingredients. The Java influences, especially y2k Date bugs but also the primitive vs. object distinction (e.g., string vs. String), were unfortunate."

I'd add to the list of "unfortunate" Java-like features that eventually made their way into JavaScript:

- Constructor functions and the new keyword, with different calling and usage semantics from factory functions.

---

[17]https://brendaneich.com/2008/04/popularity/

- A `class` keyword with single-ancestor `extends` as the primary inheritance mechanism.
- The user's tendency to think of a `class` as if it's a static type (it's not).

My advice: Avoid those whenever it's practical in your own code. When you're contributing to code that doesn't belong to you, adopt the "when in Rome" mantra. Do as the Romans do.

We're lucky that JavaScript ended up being such a capable language, because it turns out that the "scripting" approach won over the "component" approach (today, Java, Flash, and ActiveX extensions are unsupported in huge numbers of installed browsers).

What we eventually ended up with was one language directly supported by the browser: JavaScript.

That means that browsers are less bloated and less buggy, because they only need to support a single set of language bindings: JavaScript's. You might be thinking that WebAssembly is an exception, but one of the design goals of WebAssembly is to share JavaScript's language bindings using a compatible Abstract Syntax Tree (AST). In fact, the first demonstrations compiled WebAssembly to a subset of JavaScript known as ASM.js.

The position as the only standard general purpose programming language for the web platform allowed JavaScript to ride the biggest language popularity wave in the history of software:

Apps ate the world, the web ate apps, and JavaScript ate the web.

By multiple[18] measures[19], JavaScript[20] is now the most popular programming language in the world.

JavaScript is not the ideal tool for functional programming, but it's a great tool for building large applications on very large, distributed teams, where different teams may have different ideas about how to build an application.

Some teams may concentrate on scripting glue, where imperative programming is particularly useful. Others may concentrate on building architectural abstractions, where a bit of (restrained, careful) OO thinking may not be a bad idea. Still others may embrace functional programming, reducing over user actions using pure functions for deterministic, testable management of application state. Members on these teams are all using the same language, meaning that they can more easily exchange ideas, learn from each other, and build on each other's work.

In JavaScript, all of these ideas can co-exist, which allows more people to embrace JavaScript, which has led to the largest open-source package registry in the world (as of February, 2017), npm[21].

---

[18]http://redmonk.com/sogrady/2016/07/20/language-rankings-6-16/
[19]http://stackoverflow.com/research/developer-survey-2016
[20]https://octoverse.github.com/
[21]https://www.npmjs.com/

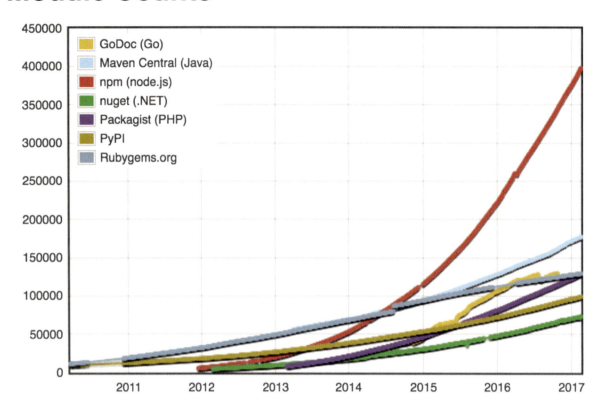

Modulecounts graph: Number of packages

The true strength of JavaScript is **diversity of thought and users** in the ecosystem. It may not be absolutely the ideal language for functional programming purists, but it may be the ideal language for working together using one language that works on just about every platform you can imagine – familiar to people coming from other popular languages such as Java, Lisp, or C. JavaScript won't feel ideally comfortable to users with any of those backgrounds, but they may feel *comfortable enough* to learn the language and become productive quickly.

I agree that JavaScript is not the best language for functional programmers. However, no other functional language can claim that it is a language that everybody can use and embrace, and as demonstrated by ES6: JavaScript can and does get better at serving the needs of users interested in functional programming. Instead of abandoning JavaScript and its incredible ecosystem used by virtually every company in the world, why not embrace it, and make it a better language for software composition incrementally?

As-is, JavaScript is already a *good enough* functional programming language, meaning that people are building all kinds of useful and interesting things in JavaScript, using functional programming techniques. Netflix (and every app built with Angular 2+) uses functional utilities based on RxJS. Facebook[22] uses the concepts of pure functions, higher-order functions, and higher order components

---

[22]https://github.com/facebook/react/wiki/sites-using-react

in React to build Facebook and Instagram. PayPal, KhanAcademy, and Flipkart[23] use Redux for state management.

They're not alone: Angular, React, Redux, and Lodash are the leading frameworks and libraries in the JavaScript application ecosystem, and all of them are heavily influenced by functional programming – or in the cases of Lodash and Redux, built for the express purpose of enabling functional programming patterns in real JavaScript applications.

"Why JavaScript?" Because JavaScript is the language that most real companies are using to build real software. Love it or hate it, JavaScript has stolen the title of "most popular functional programming language" from Lisp, which was the standard bearer for decades. True, Haskell is a much more suitable standard bearer for functional programming concepts today, but people just aren't building as many real applications in Haskell.

At any given moment, there are close to a hundred thousand JavaScript job openings in the United States, and hundreds of thousands more world-wide. Learning Haskell will teach you a lot about functional programming, but learning JavaScript will teach you a lot about building production apps for real jobs.

Apps ate the world, the web ate apps, and JavaScript ate the web.

---

[23]https://github.com/reactjs/redux/issues/310

Pure Functions

Pure functions are essential for a variety of purposes, including functional programming, concurrency, and reliable UX components. But what does "pure function" mean?

Before we can tackle what a pure function is, it's probably a good idea to take a closer look at functions. There may be a different way to look at them that will make functional programming easier to understand.

What is a Function?

A function is a process which takes some input, called arguments, and produces some output called a return value. Functions may serve the following purposes:

- **Mapping**: Produce some output based on given inputs. A function maps input values to output values.
- **Procedures**: A function may be called to perform a sequence of steps. The sequence is known as a procedure, and programming in this style is known as procedural programming.
- **I/O**: Some functions exist to communicate with other parts of the system, such as the screen, storage, system logs, or network.

Mapping

Pure functions are all about mapping. Functions map input arguments to return values, meaning that for each set of inputs, there exists an output. A function will take the inputs and return the corresponding output.

`Math.max()` takes numbers as arguments and returns the largest number:

```
1  Math.max(2, 8, 5); // 8
```

In this example, 2, 8, & 5 are arguments. They're values passed into the function.

`Math.max()` is a function that takes any number of arguments and returns the largest argument value. In this case, the largest number we passed in was 8, and that's the number that got returned.

Functions are really important in computing and math. They help us process data in useful ways. Good programmers give functions descriptive names so that when we see the code, we can see the function names and understand what the function does.

Math has functions, too, and they work a lot like functions in JavaScript. You've probably seen functions in algebra. They look something like this:

```
1  f(x) = 2x
```

Which means that we're declaring a function called f and it takes an argument called x and multiplies x by 2.

To use this function, we simply provide a value for x:

```
1  f(2)
```

In algebra, this means exactly the same thing as writing 4, so any place you see `f(2)` you can substitute 4. This property is called **referential transparency**.

Now let's convert that function to JavaScript:

```
1  const double = x => x * 2;
```

You can examine the function's output using `console.log()`:

```
1  console.log( double(5) ); // 10
```

Remember when I said that in math functions, you could replace `f(2)` with 4? In this case, the JavaScript engine replaces `double(5)` with the answer, 10.

So, `console.log( double(5) );` is the same as `console.log(10);`

This is true because `double()` is a pure function, but if `double()` had side-effects, such as saving the value to disk or logging to the console, you couldn't simply replace `double(5)` with `10` without changing the meaning.

If you want **referential transparency**, you need to use pure functions.

Pure Functions

A pure function is a function which:

1. Given the same input, will always return the same output.
2. Produces no side effects.

A dead giveaway that a function is impure is if it makes sense to call it without using its return value. For pure functions, that's a noop.

I recommend that you favor pure functions. Meaning, if it is practical to implement a program requirement using pure functions, you should use them over other options. Pure functions take some input and return some output based on that input. They are the simplest reusable building blocks of code in a program. Perhaps the most important design principle in computer science is KISS (Keep It Simple, Stupid). I prefer "**K**eep It Stupid Simple". Pure functions are stupid simple in the best possible way.

Pure functions have many beneficial properties, and form the foundation of functional programming. Pure functions are completely independent of outside state, and as such, they are immune to entire classes of bugs that have to do with shared mutable state. Their independent nature also makes them great candidates for parallel processing across many CPUs, and across entire distributed computing clusters, which makes them essential for many types of scientific and resource-intensive computing tasks.

Pure functions are also extremely independent—easy to move around, refactor, and reorganize in your code, making your programs more flexible and adaptable to future changes.

The Trouble with Shared State

Several years ago I was working on an app that allowed users to search a database for musical artists and load the artist's music playlist into a web player. This was around the time Google auto-complete launched. AJAX-powered autocomplete was suddenly all the rage.

The only problem was that users often type faster than an API autocomplete search response can be returned, which caused some strange bugs. It would trigger race conditions, where newer suggestions would be replaced by outdated suggestions.

Why did that happen? Because each AJAX success handler was given access to directly update the suggestion list that was displayed to users. The slowest AJAX request would always win the user's attention by blindly replacing results, even when those replaced results may have been newer.

To fix the problem, I created a suggestion manager—a single source of truth to manage the state of the query suggestions. It was aware of a currently pending AJAX request, and when the user typed something new, the pending AJAX request would be canceled before a new request was issued, so only a single response handler at a time would ever be able to trigger a UI state update.

Any sort of asynchronous operation or concurrency could cause similar race conditions. Race conditions happen if output is dependent on the sequence of uncontrollable events (such as network, device latency, user input, randomness, and so on). In fact, if you're using shared state and that state is reliant on sequences which vary depending on indeterministic factors, for all intents and purposes, the output is impossible to predict, and that means it's impossible to properly test or fully understand. As Martin Odersky (creator of Scala) puts it:

> "Non-determinism = parallel processing + mutable state"

Program determinism is usually a desirable property in computing. Maybe you think you're OK because JS runs in a single thread, and as such, is immune to parallel processing concerns, but as the AJAX example demonstrates, a single threaded JS engine does not imply that there is no concurrency.

On the contrary, there are many sources of concurrency in JavaScript. API I/O, event listeners, web workers, iframes, and timeouts can all introduce nondeterminism into your program. Combine that with shared state, and you've got a recipe for bugs.

Pure functions can help you avoid those kinds of bugs.

Same Input, Same Output

With our `double()` function, you can replace the function call with the result, and the program will mean the same thing—`double(5)` will always mean the same thing as `10` in your program, regardless of context, no matter how many times you call it or when.

But you can't say the same thing about all functions. Some functions rely on information other than the arguments you pass in to produce results.

Consider this example:

```
1  Math.random(); // => 0.4011148700956255
2  Math.random(); // => 0.8533405303023756
3  Math.random(); // => 0.3550692005082965
```

Even though we didn't pass any arguments into any of the function calls, they all produced different output, meaning that `Math.random()` is not pure.

`Math.random()` produces a new random number between 0 and 1 every time you run it, so clearly you couldn't just replace it with `0.4011148700956255` without changing the meaning of the program.

That would produce the same result every time. When we ask the computer for a random number, it usually means that we want a different result than we got the last time. What's the point of a pair of dice with the same numbers printed on every side?

Sometimes we have to ask the computer for the current time:

```
1  const time = () => new Date().toLocaleTimeString();
2  time(); // => "5:15:45 PM"
```

What would happen if you replaced the `time()` function call with the current time?

It would always say it's the same time: the time that the function call got replaced. In other words, if you ran it every millisecond, it could only produce the correct output once per day.

So clearly, `time()` isn't like our `double()` function.

A function is only pure if given the same input, it will always produce the same output. You may remember this rule from algebra class: the same input values will always map to the same output value. However, many input values may map to the same output value. For example, the following function is pure:

```
1  const highpass = (cutoff, value) => value >= cutoff;
```

The same input values will always map to the same output value:

```
1  highpass(5, 5); // => true
2  highpass(5, 5); // => true
3  highpass(5, 5); // => true
```

Many input values may map to the same output value:

```
1  highpass(5, 123); // true
2  highpass(5, 6);   // true
3  highpass(5, 18);  // true
4
5  highpass(5, 1);   // false
6  highpass(5, 3);   // false
7  highpass(5, 4);   // false
```

A pure function must not rely on any external mutable state, because it would no longer be deterministic or referentially transparent.

No Side Effects

A pure function produces no side effects, which means that it can't alter any external state.

Immutability

JavaScript's object arguments are references, which means that if a function were to mutate a property on an object or array parameter, that would mutate state that is accessible outside the function. Pure functions must not mutate external state.

```
1   // impure addToCart mutates existing cart
2   const addToCart = (cart, item, quantity) => {
3     cart.items.push({
4       item,
5       quantity
6     });
7     return cart;
8   };
9
10  const originalCart =     {
```

```
11      items: []
12    };
13
14    const newCart = addToCart(
15      originalCart,
16      {
17        name: "Digital SLR Camera",
18        price: '1495'
19      },
20      1
21    );
22
23    console.log(
24      // pretty print originalCart to the console
25      JSON.stringify(originalCart, undefined, 2)
26    );
```

Logs:

```
 1  {
 2    "items": [
 3      {
 4        "item": {
 5          "name": "Digital SLR Camera",
 6          "price": "1495"
 7        },
 8        "quantity": 1
 9      }
10    ]
11  }
```

It works by passing in a cart, and item to add to that cart, and an item quantity. The function then returns the same cart, with the item added to it.

The problem with this is that we've just mutated some shared state. Other functions may be relying on that cart object state to be what it was before the function was called, and now that we've mutated that shared state, we have to worry about what impact it will have on the program logic if we change the order in which functions have been called. Refactoring the code could result in bugs popping up, which could screw up orders, and result in unhappy customers.

If your software is relying on your state updates to be pure, this could cause bugs. For example, if your view compares the next state to the previous state before rendering so that it can skip rendering when the state hasn't changed, this mutating version will never update the view, even though the state has actually changed.

Now consider this version:

```javascript
// Pure addToCart() returns a new cart
// It does not mutate the original.
const addToCart = (cart, item, quantity) => {
  return {
    ...cart,
    items: cart.items.concat([{
      item,
      quantity
    }]),
  };
};

const originalCart =     {
  items: []
};

const newCart = addToCart(
  originalCart,
  {
    name: "Digital SLR Camera",
    price: '1495'
  },
  1
);

console.log(
  // pretty print originalCart to the console
  JSON.stringify(originalCart, undefined, 2)
);
```

Logs:

```
{
  "items": []
}
```

And `newCart` contains the new item:

```json
{
  "items": [
    {
      "item": {
        "name": "Digital SLR Camera",
        "price": "1495"
      },
      "quantity": 1
    }
  ]
}
```

Conclusion

A **pure function** is a function which, given the same state, always returns the same output, and has no side-effects.

Pure functions are the simplest kind of function. You should prefer them whenever they are practical. They are deterministic, which makes them easy to understand, debug, and test. Determinism also makes them immune to entire classes of bugs dealing with shared mutable state, side-effects, race conditions, and so on.

An expression is **referentially transparent** if you can replace the expression with its corresponding value without changing the meaning of the program.

Pure functions can be used to optimize software performance. For instance, rendering a view is often an expensive operation, which can be skipped if the data underlying the view has not changed. When pure functions are used for view state updates, you can check to see whether or not a view should be rerendered by comparing the previous state to the new state.

What is Functional Programming?

Functional programming has become a really hot topic in the JavaScript world. Just a few years ago, few JavaScript programmers even knew what functional programming is, but every large application codebase I've seen in the past 3 years makes heavy use of functional programming ideas.

Functional programming (often abbreviated FP) is a programming paradigm where applications are composed using pure functions, avoiding shared mutable state and side-effects. Functional programming is usually more declarative than imperative, meaning that we express what to do rather than how to do it.

Other examples of programming paradigms include object oriented programming, where data and behaviors are colocated, and procedural programming, which is an imperative style grouping algorithms into procedures which tend to rely on shared mutable state.

Functional code tends to be more concise, more predictable, and easier to test than imperative or object oriented code—but if you're unfamiliar with it and the common patterns associated with it, functional code can also seem a lot more dense, and the related literature can be impenetrable to newcomers.

If you start googling functional programming terms, you're going to quickly hit a brick wall of academic lingo that can be very intimidating. To say it has a learning curve is a serious understatement. But if you've been programming in JavaScript for a while, chances are good that you've used a lot of functional programming concepts & utilities in your real software.

Don't let all the new words scare you away. It's a lot easier than it sounds.

The hardest part is wrapping your head around all the unfamiliar vocabulary. There are a lot of ideas in the innocent looking definition above which all need to be understood before you can begin to grasp the meaning of functional programming:

- Pure functions
- Function composition
- Avoid shared state
- Avoid mutating state
- Avoid side effects
- Declarative vs imperative

In other words, if you want to know what functional programming means in practice, you have to start with an understanding of those core concepts.

Pure Functions

A pure function is a function which:

- Given the same inputs, always returns the same output, and
- Has no side-effects

Pure functions have lots of properties that are important in functional programming, including referential transparency (you can replace a function call with its resulting value without changing the meaning of the program).

Function Composition

Function composition is the process of combining two or more functions in order to produce a new function or perform some computation. For example, the composition f . g (the dot means "composed with") is equivalent to f(g(x)) in JavaScript. Understanding function composition is an important step towards understanding how software is constructed using the functional programming. Read "What is Function Composition?" for more.

Shared State

Shared state is any variable, object, or memory space that exists in a shared scope, or as the property of an object being passed between scopes. A shared scope can include global scope or closure scopes. Often, in object oriented programming, objects are shared between scopes by adding properties to other objects.

For example, a computer game might have a master game object, with characters and game items stored as properties owned by that object. Functional programming avoids shared state—instead relying on immutable data structures and pure calculations to derive new data from existing data.

The problem with shared state is that in order to understand the effects of a function, you have to know the entire history of every shared variable that the function uses or affects.

Imagine you have a user object which needs saving. Your `saveUser()` function makes a request to an API on the server. While that's happening, the user changes their profile picture with `updateAvatar()` and triggers another `saveUser()` request. On save, the server sends back a canonical user object that should replace whatever is in memory in order to sync up with changes that happen on the server or in response to other API calls.

Unfortunately, the second response gets received before the first response, so when the first (now outdated) response gets returned, the new profile pic gets wiped out in memory and replaced with the old one. This is an example of a race condition—a very common bug associated with shared state.

Another common problem associated with shared state is that changing the order in which functions are called can cause a cascade of failures because functions which act on shared state are timing dependent. With shared state, the order in which function calls are made changes the result of the function calls:

```javascript
// Shared state
const x = {
  val: 2
};

// Mutates shared state
const x1 = () => x.val += 1;

// Mutates shared state
const x2 = () => x.val *= 2;

x1();
x2();

console.log(x.val); // 6

// This example is exactly equivalent to the above, except...
const y = {
  val: 2
};

const y1 = () => y.val += 1;

const y2 = () => y.val *= 2;

// ...the order of the function calls is reversed...
y2();
y1();

// ... which changes the resulting value:
console.log(y.val); // 5
```

When you avoid shared state, the timing and order of function calls don't change the result of calling the function. With pure functions, given the same input, you'll always get the same output. This makes function calls completely independent of other function calls, which can radically simplify changes and refactoring. A change in one function, or the timing of a function call won't ripple out and break other parts of the program.

```
const x = {
  val: 2
};

const inc = x => ({...x, val: x.val + 1});
const double = x => ({...x, val: x.val * 2});

console.log(inc(double(x)).val); // 5

const y = {
  val: 2
};

/*
Because the functions don't mutate, you can call
these functions as many times as you want, in any order,
without changing the result of other function calls.
*/

// These calls do nothing:
inc(y);
double(y);

console.log(inc(double(y)).val); // 5
```

In the example above, we use object spread (`{...x, val: x.val + 1}`) to copy the properties of x instead of mutating it in place.

If you look closely at the `console.log()` statements in this example, you should notice something I've mentioned already: function composition. Recall from earlier, function composition looks like this: `f(g(x))`. In this case, we replace `f()` and `g()` with `inc()` and `double()` for the composition: x1 . x2.

Of course, if you change the order of the composition, the output will change. Order of operations still matters. `f(g(x))` is not always equal to `g(f(x))`, but what doesn't matter anymore is what happens to variables outside the function—and that's a big deal. With impure functions, it's impossible to fully understand what a function does unless you know the entire history of every variable that the function uses or affects.

Remove function call timing dependency, and you eliminate an entire class of potential bugs.

Immutability

An immutable object is an object that can't be modified after it's created. Conversely, a mutable object is any object which can be modified after it's created.

Immutability is a central concept of functional programming because without it, the data flow in your program is lossy. State history is abandoned, and strange bugs can creep into your software.

In JavaScript, it's important not to confuse `const`, with immutability. `const` creates a variable name binding which can't be reassigned after creation. `const` does not create immutable objects. You can't change the object that the binding refers to, but you can still change the properties of the object, which means that bindings created with const are mutable, not immutable.

Immutable objects can't be changed at all. You can make a value truly immutable by deep freezing the object. JavaScript has a method that freezes an object one-level deep:

```javascript
const a = Object.freeze({
  foo: 'Hello',
  bar: 'world',
  baz: '!'
});

a.foo = 'Goodbye';
// Error: Cannot assign to read only property 'foo' of object Object
```

But frozen objects are only superficially immutable. For example, the following object is mutable:

```javascript
const a = Object.freeze({
  foo: { greeting: 'Hello' },
  bar: 'world',
  baz: '!'
});

a.foo.greeting = 'Goodbye';

console.log(`${ a.foo.greeting }, ${ a.bar }${a.baz}`);
// 'Goodbye, world!'
```

As you can see, the top level primitive properties of a frozen object can't change, but any property which is also an object (including arrays, etc.) can still be mutated—so even frozen objects are not immutable unless you walk the whole object tree and freeze every object property.

In many functional programming languages, there are special immutable data structures called trie data structures (pronounced "tree") which are effectively deep frozen—meaning that no property can change, regardless of the level of the property in the object hierarchy.

Tries use structural sharing to share reference memory locations for all the parts of the object which are unchanged after a "mutation", which uses less memory, and enables significant performance improvements for some kinds of operations.

For example, you can use identity comparisons at the root of an object tree for comparisons. If the identity is the same, you don't have to walk the whole tree checking for differences.

There are several libraries in JavaScript which take advantage of tries, including Immutable.js[24] and Mori[25].

Side Effects

A side effect is any application state change that is observable outside the called function other than its return value. Side effects include:

- Modifying any external variable or object property (e.g., a global variable, or a variable in the parent function scope chain)
- Logging to the console
- Writing to the screen
- Writing to a file
- Writing to the network
- Triggering any external process
- Calling any other functions with side-effects

Side effects are mostly avoided in functional programming, which makes the effects of a program easier to extend, refactor, debug, test, and maintain. This is the reason that most frameworks encourage users to manage state and component rendering in separate, loosely coupled modules.

Reusability Through Higher Order Functions

A **higher order function** is any function which takes a function as an argument, returns a function, or both. Higher order functions are often used to:

- Abstract or isolate actions, effects, or async flow control using callback functions, promises, monads, etc.
- Create utilities which can act on a wide variety of data types
- Partially apply a function to its arguments or create a curried function for the purpose of reuse or function composition
- Take a list of functions and return some composition of those input functions

---

[24]https://facebook.github.io/immutable-js/
[25]https://github.com/swannodette/mori

Functional programming tends to reuse a common set of functional utilities to process data. Object oriented programming tends to colocate methods and data in objects. In most object-oriented software, those colocated methods can only operate on the type of data they were designed to operate on, and often only the data contained in that specific object instance.

In functional programming, any type of data is fair game. The same map() utility can map over objects, strings, numbers, or any other data type because it takes a function as an argument which appropriately handles the given data type. FP pulls off its generic utility trickery using higher order functions and parameter substitution.

JavaScript has first class functions, which allows us to treat functions as data—assign them to variables, pass them to other functions, return them from functions, etc.

Containers, Functors, Lists, and Streams

A **functor data structure** is a data structure that can be mapped over (e.g., [1,2,3].map(x => x * 2)). In other words, it's a container which has an interface which can be used to apply a function to the values inside it. When you see the word functor, you should think "mappable".

Earlier we learned that the same map() utility can act on a variety of data types. It does that by lifting the mapping operation to work with a functor API. The important flow control operations used by map() take advantage of that interface.

In the case of Array.prototype.map(), the container is an array, but other data structures can be functors, too—as long as they supply the mapping API.

Let's look at how Array.prototype.map() allows you to abstract the data type from the mapping utility to make map() usable with any data type. We'll create a simple double() mapping that simply multiplies any passed in values by 2:

```
const double = n => n * 2;
const doubleMap = numbers => numbers.map(double);
console.log(doubleMap([2, 3, 4])); // [ 4, 6, 8 ]
```

What if we want to operate on targets in a game to double the number of points they award? All we have to do is make a subtle change to the double() function that we pass into map(), and everything still works:

```javascript
const double = n => n.points * 2;

const doubleMap = numbers => numbers.map(double);

console.log(doubleMap([
  { name: 'ball', points: 2 },
  { name: 'coin', points: 3 },
  { name: 'candy', points: 4}
])); // [ 4, 6, 8 ]
```

The concept of using abstractions like functors and higher order functions in order to use generic utility functions to manipulate any number of different data types is important in functional programming. You'll see a similar concept applied in all sorts of different ways.

> "A list expressed over time is a stream."

Arrays and functors are not the only way this concept of containers and values in containers applies. For example, an array is just a list of things. A list expressed over time is a stream—so you can apply the same kinds of utilities to process streams of incoming events—something that you'll see a lot when you start building real software with FP.

Declarative vs Imperative

Functional programming is a declarative paradigm, meaning that the program logic is expressed without explicitly describing the flow control.

- **Imperative** programs spend lines of code describing the specific steps used to achieve the desired results—the flow control: *How to do things.*
- **Declarative** programs abstract the flow control process (the how gets abstracted away), and instead spend lines of code describing the data flow: *What to do.*

For example, this imperative mapping takes an array of numbers and returns a new array with each number multiplied by 2:

```
1  const doubleMap = numbers => {
2    const doubled = [];
3    for (let i = 0; i < numbers.length; i++) {
4      doubled.push(numbers[i] * 2);
5    }
6    return doubled;
7  };
8
9  console.log(doubleMap([2, 3, 4])); // [4, 6, 8]
```

This declarative mapping does the same thing, but abstracts the flow control away using the functional Array.prototype.map() utility, which allows you to more clearly express the flow of data:

```
1  const doubleMap = numbers => numbers.map(n => n * 2);
2
3  console.log(doubleMap([2, 3, 4])); // [4, 6, 8]
```

Imperative code frequently utilizes statements. A **statement** is a piece of code which performs some action. Examples of commonly used statements include `for`, `if`, `switch`, `throw`, etc.

Declarative code relies more on expressions. An **expression** is a piece of code which evaluates to some value. Expressions are usually some combination of function calls, values, and operators which are evaluated to produce the resulting value.

These are all examples of expressions:

- `2 * 2`
- `doubleMap([2, 3, 4])`
- `Math.max(4, 3, 2)`
- `'a' + 'b' + 'c'`
- `{...a, ...b, ...c}`

Usually in code, you'll see expressions being assigned to an identifier (variable name), returned from functions, or passed into a function. Before being assigned, returned, or passed, the expression is first evaluated, and the resulting value is used.

Conclusion

Functional programming favors:

- **Pure functions** over shared state and side effects
- **Immutability** over mutable data

- **Function composition** over imperative flow control
- **Generic** utilities that act on many data types over object methods that only operate on their colocated data
- **Declarative** over imperative code (what to do, rather than how to do it)
- **Expressions** over statements

A Functional Programmer's Introduction to JavaScript

For those unfamiliar with JavaScript or ES6+, this is intended as a brief introduction. Whether you're a beginner or experienced JavaScript developer, you may learn something new. The following is only meant to scratch the surface and get you excited. If you want to know more, you'll just have to explore deeper. There's a lot more ahead.

The best way to learn to code is to code. I recommend that you follow along using an interactive JavaScript programming environment such as CodePen[26] or the Babel REPL[27].

Alternatively, you can get away with using the Node or browser console REPLs.

Expressions and Values

An **expression** is a chunk of code that evaluates to a value.

The following are all valid expressions in JavaScript:

```
7;

7 + 1; // 8

7 * 2; // 14

'Hello'; // Hello
```

The value of an expression can be given a name. When you do so, the expression is evaluated first, and the resulting value is assigned to the name. For this, we'll use the `const` keyword. It's not the only way, but it's the one you'll use most, so we'll stick with `const` for now:

```
const hello = 'Hello';
hello; // Hello
```

---

[26]https://codepen.io
[27]https://babeljs.io/repl/

var, let, and const

JavaScript supports two more variable declaration keywords: `var`, and `let`. I like to think of them in terms of order of selection. By default, I select the strictest declaration: `const`. A variable declared with the `const` keyword can't be reassigned. The final value must be assigned at declaration time. This may sound rigid, but the restriction is a good thing. It's a signal that tells you, "the value assigned to this name is not going to change". It helps you fully understand what the name means right away, without needing to read the whole function or block scope.

Sometimes it's useful to reassign variables. For example, if you're using manual, imperative iteration rather than a more functional approach, you can iterate a counter assigned with `let`.

Because `var` tells you the least about the variable, it is the weakest signal. Since I started using ES6, I have never intentionally declared a `var` in a real software project.

Be aware that once a variable is declared with `let` or `const`, any attempt to declare it again will result in an error. If you prefer more experimental flexibility in the REPL (Read, Eval, Print Loop) environment, you may use `var` instead of `const` to declare variables. Redeclaring `var` is allowed.

This text will use `const` in order to get you in the habit of defaulting to `const` for actual programs, but feel free to substitute `var` for the purpose of interactive experimentation.

Types

So far we've seen two types: numbers and strings. JavaScript also has booleans (`true` or `false`), arrays, objects, and more. We'll get to other types later.

An **array** is an ordered list of values. Think of it as a box that can hold many items. Here's the **array literal notation**:

```
1  [1, 2, 3];
```

Of course, that's an expression which can be given a name:

```
1  const arr = [1, 2, 3];
```

An **object** in JavaScript is a collection of key: value pairs. It also has a literal notation:

```
1  {
2    key: 'value'
3  };
```

And of course, you can assign an object to a name:

```
1  const foo = {
2    bar: 'bar'
3  };
```

If you want to assign existing variables to object property keys of the same name, there's a shortcut for that. You can just type the variable name instead of providing both a key and a value:

```
1  const a = 'a';
2  const oldA = { a: a }; // long, redundant way
3  const oA = { a }; // short an sweet!
```

Just for fun, let's do that again:

```
1  const b = 'b';
2  const oB = { b };
```

Objects can be easily composed together into new objects:

```
1  const c = {...oA, ...oB}; // { a: 'a', b: 'b' }
```

Those dots are the **object spread operator**. It iterates over the properties in oA and assigns them to the new object, then does the same for oB, overriding any keys that already exist on the new object. As of this writing, object spread is a new, experimental feature that may not be available in all the popular browsers yet, but if it's not working for you, there is a substitute: Object.assign():

```
1  const d = Object.assign({}, oA, oB); // { a: 'a', b: 'b' }
```

Only a little more typing in the Object.assign() example, and if you're composing lots of objects, it may even save you some typing. Note that when you use Object.assign(), you must pass a destination object as the first parameter. It is the object that properties will be copied to. If you forget, and omit the destination object, the object you pass in the first argument **will be mutated**.

In my experience, mutating an existing object rather than creating a new object is **usually a bug**. At the very least, it is error-prone. Be careful with Object.assign().

Destructuring

Both objects and arrays support destructuring, meaning that you can extract values from them and assign them to named variables:

```
1  const [t, u] = ['a', 'b'];
2  t; // 'a'
3  u; // 'b'
```

```
1  const blep = {
2    blop: 'blop'
3  };
4
5  // The following is equivalent to:
6  // const blop = blep.blop;
7  const { blop } = blep;
8  blop; // 'blop'
```

As with the array example above, you can destructure to multiple assignments at once. Here's a line you'll see in lots of Redux projects:

```
1  const { type, payload } = action;
```

Here's how it's used in the context of a reducer (much more on that topic coming later):

```
1  const myReducer = (state = {}, action = {}) => {
2    const { type, payload } = action;
3    switch (type) {
4      case 'FOO': return Object.assign({}, state, payload);
5      default: return state;
6    }
7  };
```

If you don't want to use a different name for the new binding, you can assign a new name:

```
1  const { blop: bloop } = blep;
2  bloop; // 'blop'
```

Read: Assign `blep.blop` as `bloop`.

Comparisons and Ternaries

You can compare values with the strict equality operator (sometimes called "triple equals"):

```
3 + 1 === 4; // true
```

There's also a sloppy equality operator. It's formally known as the "Equal" operator. Informally, "double equals". Double equals has a valid use-case or two, but it's almost always better to default to the === operator, instead.

Other comparison operators include:

- \> Greater than
- < Less than
- \>= Greater than or equal to
- <= Less than or equal to
- != Not equal
- !== Not strict equal
- && Logical and
- || Logical or

A ternary expression is an expression that lets you ask a question using a comparator, and evaluates to a different answer depending on whether or not the expression is truthy:

```
14 - 7 === 7 ? 'Yep!' : 'Nope.'; // Yep!
14 - 7 === 53 ? 'Yep!' : 'Nope.'; // Nope.
```

Functions

JavaScript has function expressions, which can be assigned to names:

```
const double = x => x * 2;
```

This means the same thing as the mathematical function $f(x) = 2x$. Spoken out loud, that function reads f of x equals 2x. This function is only interesting when you apply it to a specific value of x. To use the function in other equations, you'd write f(2), which has the same meaning as 4.

In other words, f(2) = 4. You can think of a math function as a mapping from inputs to outputs. f(x) in this case is a mapping of input values for x to corresponding output values equal to the product of the input value and 2.

In JavaScript, the value of a function expression is the function itself:

```
double; // [Function: double]
```

You can see the function definition using the .toString() method:

```
1  double.toString(); // 'x => x * 2'
```

If you want to apply a function to some arguments, you must **invoke** it with a **function call**. A function call applies a function to its arguments and evaluates to a **return value**.

You can invoke a function using `<functionName>(argument1, argument2, ...rest)`. For example, to invoke our double function, just add the parentheses and pass in a value to double:

```
1  double(2); // 4
```

Unlike some functional languages, those parentheses are meaningful. Without them, the function won't be called:

```
1  double 4; // SyntaxError: Unexpected number
```

Signatures

Functions have signatures, which consist of:

1. An *optional* function name.
2. A list of parameter types, in parentheses. The parameters may optionally be named.
3. The type of the return value.

Type signatures don't need to be specified in JavaScript. The JavaScript engine will figure out the types at runtime. If you provide enough clues, the signature can also be inferred by developer tools such as IDEs (Integrated Development Environment) and Tern.js[28] using data flow analysis.

JavaScript lacks its own function signature notation, so there are a few competing standards: JSDoc has been very popular historically, but it's awkwardly verbose, and nobody bothers to keep the doc comments up-to-date with the code, so many JS developers have stopped using it.

TypeScript and Flow are currently the big contenders. I'm not sure how to express everything I need in either of those, so I use Rtype[29], for documentation purposes only. Some people fall back on Haskell's curry-only Hindley-Milner types[30]. I'd love to see a good notation system standardized for JavaScript, if only for documentation purposes, but I don't think any of the current solutions are up to the task, at present. For now, squint and do your best to keep up with the weird rtype signatures which probably look slightly different from whatever you're using.

---

[28]http://ternjs.net/
[29]https://github.com/ericelliott/rtype
[30]http://web.cs.wpi.edu/~cs4536/c12/milner-damas_principal_types.pdf

```
1    functionName(param1: Type, param2: Type) => ReturnType
```

Signatures start with a function name (`functionName` above), followed by an open parenthesis, followed by an *optional* parameter name with a colon on the end (`param1`), followed by the type (`Type`). The type may be a type variable (conventionally one letter, lowercase), or a concrete type (full word, spelled out, capitalized). The return type is identified by the fat arrow (=>) pointing at the return type (`ReturnType`), which, like the parameter types, may also be a `name: Type` pair.

The signature for double is:

```
1    double(x: Number) => Number
```

But what if we want it to accept objects as well?

```
1    const one = {
2      name: 'One',
3      valueOf: () => 1
4    };
5
6    double(one); // 2
```

In that case, we'll need to change the signature to use a type variable:

```
1    double(x: n) => Number
```

If the name of the variable is not important, we'll sometimes leave it out:

```
1    double(n) => Number
```

In spite of the fact that JavaScript doesn't require signatures to be annotated, knowing what signatures *are* and what they *mean* will still be important in order to communicate efficiently about how functions are used, and how functions are composed. Most reusable function composition utilities require you to pass functions which share the same type signature, so we need a way to express what those signatures are. The Rtype[31] signatures you'll encounter in this text mix the best features of Haskell and TypeScript's type notations in order to match the expressive power of the JavaScript language itself (which both Haskell and TypeScript's notations fail to do well).

Default Parameter Values

JavaScript supports default parameter values. The following function works as an identity function (a function which returns the same value you pass in), unless you call it with `false`, `null`, `undefined`, or simply pass no argument at all – then it returns zero, instead:

---
[31]https://github.com/ericelliott/rtype

```
1  const orZero = (n = 0) => n;
```

To set a default, simply assign it to the parameter with the = operator in the function signature, as in n = 0, above. When you assign default values in this way, type inference tools such as Tern.js[32], Flow, or TypeScript can infer the type signature of your function automatically, even if you don't explicitly declare type annotations.

The result is that, with the right plugins installed in your editor or IDE, you'll be able to see function signatures displayed inline as you're typing function calls. You'll also be able to understand how to use a function at a glance based on its call signature. Using default assignments wherever it makes sense can help you write more self-documenting code.

> Note: Parameters with defaults don't count toward the function's .length property, which will throw off utilities such as autocurry which depend on the .length value. Some curry utilities (such as lodash/curry) allow you to pass a custom arity to work around this limitation if you bump into it.

Named Arguments

JavaScript functions can take object literals as arguments and use destructuring assignment in the parameter signature in order to achieve the equivalent of named arguments. Notice, you can also assign default values to parameters using the default parameter feature:

```
1   const createUser = ({
2     name = 'Anonymous',
3     avatarThumbnail = '/avatars/anonymous.png'
4   }) => ({
5     name,
6     avatarThumbnail
7   });
8
9   const george = createUser({
10    name: 'George',
11    avatarThumbnail: 'avatars/shades-emoji.png'
12  });
13
14  george;
15  /*
16  {
17    name: 'George',
18    avatarThumbnail: 'avatars/shades-emoji.png'
19  }
20  */
```

---

[32]http://ternjs.net/

Rest and Spread

A common feature of functions in JavaScript is the ability to gather together a group of remaining arguments in the functions signature using the rest operator: ...

For example, the following function simply discards the first argument and returns the rest as an array:

```
1  const aTail = (head, ...tail) => tail;
2  aTail(1, 2, 3); // [2, 3]
```

Rest gathers individual elements together into an array. Spread does the opposite: it spreads the elements from an array to individual elements. Consider this:

```
1  const shiftToLast = (head, ...tail) => [...tail, head];
2  shiftToLast(1, 2, 3); // [2, 3, 1]
```

Arrays in JavaScript have an iterator that gets invoked when the spread operator is used. For each item in the array, the iterator delivers a value. In the expression, [...tail, head], the iterator copies each element in order from the tail array into the new array created by the surrounding literal notation. Since the head is already an individual element, we just plop it onto the end of the array and we're done.

Currying

A **curried function** is a function that takes multiple parameters one at a time: It takes a parameter, and returns a function that takes the next parameter, and so on until all parameters have been supplied, at which point, the application is completed and the final value returned.

Curry and partial application can be enabled by returning another function:

```
1  const gte = cutoff => n => n >= cutoff;
2  const gte4 = gte(4); // gte() returns a new function
```

You don't have to use arrow functions. JavaScript also has a function keyword. We're using arrow functions because the function keyword is a lot more typing. This is equivalent to the gte() definition, above:

```javascript
function gte (cutoff) {
  return function (n) {
    return n >= cutoff;
  };
};
```

The arrow in JavaScript roughly means "function". There are some important differences in function behavior depending on which kind of function you use (=> lacks its own `this`, and can't be used as a constructor), but we'll get to those differences when we get there. For now, when you see `x => x`, think "a function that takes x and returns x". So you can read `const gte = cutoff => n => n >= cutoff;` as:

"`gte` is a function which takes `cutoff` and returns a function which takes `n` and returns the result of `n >= cutoff`".

Since `gte()` returns a function, you can use it to create a more specialized function:

```javascript
const gte4 = gte(4);

gte4(6); // true
gte4(3); // false
```

Autocurry lets you curry functions automatically, for maximal flexibility. Say you have a function `add3()`:

```javascript
const add3 = curry((a, b, c) => a + b + c);
```

With autocurry, you can use it in several different ways, and it will return the right thing depending on how many arguments you pass in:

```javascript
add3(1, 2, 3); // 6
add3(1, 2)(3); // 6
add3(1)(2, 3); // 6
add3(1)(2)(3); // 6
```

Sorry Haskell fans, JavaScript lacks a built-in autocurry mechanism, but you can import one from Lodash:

```
$ npm install --save lodash
```

Then, in your modules:

```
1  import curry from 'lodash/curry';
```

Or, you can use the following magic spell:

```
1  // Tiny, recursive autocurry
2  const curry = (
3    f, arr = []
4  ) => (...args) => (
5    a => a.length === f.length ?
6      f(...a) :
7      curry(f, a)
8  )([...arr, ...args]);
```

Function Composition

Of course you can compose functions. Function composition is the process of passing the return value of one function as an argument to another function. In mathematical notation:

```
1  f . g
```

Which translates to this in JavaScript:

```
1  f(g(x))
```

It's evaluated from the inside out:

1. x is evaluated
2. g() is applied to x
3. f() is applied to the return value of g(x)

For example:

```
1  const inc = n => n + 1;
2  inc(double(2)); // 5
```

The value 2 is passed into double(), which produces 4. 4 is passed into inc() which evaluates to 5.

You can pass any expression as an argument to a function. The expression will be evaluated before the function is applied:

```
inc(double(2) * double(2)); // 17
```

Since `double(2)` evaluates to 4, you can read that as `inc(4 * 4)` which evaluates to `inc(16)` which then evaluates to 17.

Function composition is central to functional programming. We'll have a lot more on it later.

Arrays

Arrays have some built-in methods. A **method** is a function associated with an object: usually a property of the associated object:

```
const arr = [1, 2, 3];
arr.map(double); // [2, 4, 6]
```

In this case, `arr` is the object, `.map()` is a property of the object with a function for a value. When you invoke it, the function gets applied to the arguments, as well as a special parameter called `this`, which gets automatically set when the method is invoked. The `this` value is how `.map()` gets access to the contents of the array.

Note that we're passing the `double` function as a value into `map` rather than calling it. That's because `map` takes a function as an argument and applies it to each item in the array. It returns a new array containing the values returned by `double()`.

Note that the original `arr` value is unchanged:

```
arr; // [1, 2, 3]
```

Method Chaining

You can also chain method calls. **Method chaining** is the process of directly calling a method on the return value of a function, without needing to refer to the return value by name:

```
const arr = [1, 2, 3];
arr.map(double).map(double); // [4, 8, 12]
```

A **predicate** is a function that returns a boolean value (`true` or `false`). The `.filter()` method takes a predicate and returns a new list, selecting only the items that pass the predicate (return `true`) to be included in the new list:

```
const gte = cutoff => n => n >= cutoff;
[2, 4, 6].filter(gte(4)); // [4, 6]
```

Frequently, you'll want to select items from a list, and then map those items to a new list:

```
const gte = cutoff => n => n >= cutoff;
[2, 4, 6].filter(gte(4)).map(double); // [8, 12]
```

Note: Later in this text, you'll see a more efficient way to select and map at the same time using something called a *transducer*, but there are other things to explore first.

Conclusion

If your head is spinning right now, don't worry. We barely scratched the surface of a lot of things that deserve a lot more exploration and consideration. We'll circle back and explore some of these topics in much more depth, soon.

Higher Order Functions

Earlier we saw examples of `.map()` and `.filter()`. Both of them take a function as an argument. They're both higher order functions. A **higher order function** is a function that takes a function as an argument, or returns a function. Higher order function is in contrast to first order functions, which don't take a function as an argument or return a function as output.

Let's look at an example of a first-order function which filters all the 4-letter words from a list of words:

```javascript
const censor = words => {
  const filtered = [];
  for (let i = 0, { length } = words; i < length; i++) {
    const word = words[i];
    if (word.length !== 4) filtered.push(word);
  }
  return filtered;
};

censor(['oops', 'gasp', 'shout', 'sun']);
// [ 'shout', 'sun' ]
```

Now what if we want to select all the words that begin with 's'? We could create another function:

```javascript
const startsWithS = words => {
  const filtered = [];
  for (let i = 0, { length } = words; i < length; i++) {
    const word = words[i];
    if (word.startsWith('s')) filtered.push(word);
  }
  return filtered;
};

startsWithS(['oops', 'gasp', 'shout', 'sun']);
// [ 'shout', 'sun' ]
```

You may already be recognizing a lot of repeated code. There's a pattern forming here that could be abstracted into a more generalized solution. These two functions have a whole lot in common. They both iterate over a list and filter it on a given condition.

Both the iteration and the filtering seem like they're begging to be abstracted so they can be shared and reused to build all sorts of similar functions. After all, selecting things from lists of things is a very common task.

Luckily for us, JavaScript has first class functions. What does that mean? Just like numbers, strings, or objects, functions can be:

- Assigned as an identifier (variable) value
- Assigned to object property values
- Passed as arguments
- Returned from functions

We can use functions just like any other value in our programs, and that makes abstraction a lot easier. For instance, we can create a function that abstracts the process of iterating over a list and accumulating a return value by passing in a function that handles *the bits that are different*. We'll call that function the *reducer*:

```javascript
const reduce = (reducer, initial, arr) => {
  // shared stuff
  let acc = initial;
  for (let i = 0, { length } = arr; i < length; i++) {

    // unique stuff in reducer call
    acc = reducer(acc, arr[i]);

    // more shared stuff
  }
  return acc;
};

reduce((acc, curr) => acc + curr, 0, [1,2,3]); // 6
```

This `reduce()` implementation takes a reducer function, an initial value for the accumulator, and an array of data to iterate over. For each item in the array, the reducer is called, passing it the accumulator and the current array element. The return value is assigned to the accumulator. When it's finished applying the reducer to all of the values in the list, the accumulated value is returned.

In the usage example, we call reduce and pass it the function, `(acc, curr) => acc + curr`, which takes the accumulator and the current value in the list and returns a new accumulated value. Next we pass an initial value, `0`, and finally, the data to iterate over.

With the iteration and value accumulation abstracted, now we can implement a more generalized `filter()` function:

```
const filter = (
  fn, arr
) => reduce((acc, curr) => fn(curr) ?
  acc.concat([curr]) :
  acc, [], arr
);
```

In the `filter()` function, everything is shared except the `fn()` function that gets passed in as an argument. That `fn()` argument is called a predicate. A **predicate** is a function that returns a boolean value.

We call `fn()` with the current value, and if the `fn(curr)` test returns `true`, we concat the `curr` value to the accumulator array. Otherwise, we just return the current accumulator value.

Now we can implement `censor()` with `filter()` to filter out 4-letter words:

```
const censor = words => filter(
  word => word.length !== 4,
  words
);
```

Wow! With all the common stuff abstracted out, `censor()` is a tiny function. And so is `startsWithS()`:

```
const startsWithS = words => filter(
  word => word.startsWith('s'),
  words
);
```

If you're paying attention, you probably know that JavaScript has already done this abstraction work for us. We have the `Array.prototype` methods, `.reduce()` and `.filter()` and `.map()` and a few more for good measure.

Higher order functions are also commonly used to abstract how to operate on different data types. For instance, `.filter()` doesn't have to operate on arrays of strings. It could just as easily filter numbers, because you can pass in a function that knows how to deal with a different data type. Remember the `highpass()` example?

```
const highpass = cutoff => n => n >= cutoff;
const gte3 = highpass(3);
[1, 2, 3, 4].filter(gte3); // [3, 4];
```

In other words, you can use higher order functions to make a function polymorphic. As you can see, higher order functions can be a whole lot more reusable and versatile than their first order cousins. Generally speaking, you'll use higher order functions in combination with very simple first order functions in your real application code.

Curry and Function Composition

With the dramatic rise of functional programming in mainstream JavaScript, curried functions have become common in many applications. It's important to understand what they are, how they work, and how to put them to good use.

What is a curried function?

A curried function is a function that takes multiple arguments *one at a time.* Given a function with 3 parameters, the curried version will take one argument and return a function that takes the next argument, which returns a function that takes the third argument. The last function returns the result of applying the function to all of its arguments.

You can do the same thing with more or fewer parameters. For example, given two numbers, a and b in curried form, return the sum of a and b:

```
1  // add = a => b => Number
2  const add = a => b => a + b;
```

To use it, we must apply **both functions**, using the function application syntax. In JavaScript, the parentheses () after the function reference triggers function invocation. When a function returns another function, the returned function can be immediately invoked by adding an extra set of parentheses:

```
1  const result = add(2)(3); // => 5
```

First, the function takes a, and then *returns a new function,* which then takes b returns the sum of a and b. Each argument is taken *one at a time.* If the function had more parameters, it could simply continue to return new functions until all of the arguments are supplied and the application can be completed.

The add function takes one argument, and then returns a **partial application** of itself with a **fixed** in the closure scope. A **closure** is a function bundled with its lexical scope. Closures are created at runtime during function creation. **Fixed** means that the variables are assigned values in the closure's bundled scope.

The parentheses in the example above represent function invocations: add is invoked with 2, which returns a partially applied function with a fixed to 2. Instead of assigning the return value to a variable or otherwise using it, we immediately invoke the returned function by passing 3 to it in parentheses, which completes the application and returns 5.

What is a partial application?

A partial application is a function which has been applied to some, but not yet all of its arguments. In other words, it's a function which has some arguments *fixed* inside its closure scope. A function with some of its parameters fixed is said to be *partially applied*.

What's the Difference?

Partial applications can take as many or as few arguments a time as desired. Curried functions on the other hand *always* return a **unary function**: a function which takes *one argument*.

All curried functions return partial applications, but not all partial applications are the result of curried functions.

The unary requirement for curried functions is an important feature.

What is point-free style?

Point-free style is a style of programming where function definitions do not make reference to the function's arguments. Let's look at function definitions in JavaScript:

```
function foo (/* parameters are declared here*/) {
  // ...
}
```

```
const foo = (/* parameters are declared here */) => // ...
```

```
const foo = function (/* parameters are declared here */) {
  // ...
}
```

How can you define functions in JavaScript without referencing the required parameters? Well, we can't use the `function` keyword, and we can't use an arrow function (`=>`) because those require any formal parameters to be declared (which would reference its arguments). So what we'll need to do instead is call a function that returns a function.

Create a function that increments whatever number you pass to it by one using point-free style. Remember, we already have a function called `add` that takes a number and returns a partially applied function with its first parameter fixed to whatever you pass in. We can use that to create a new function called `inc()`:

```
1  // inc = n => Number
2  // Adds 1 to any number.
3  const inc = add(1);
4  inc(3); // => 4
```

This gets interesting as a mechanism for generalization and specialization. The returned function is just a *specialized version* of the more general add() function. We can use add() to create as many specialized versions as we want:

```
1  const inc10 = add(10);
2  const inc20 = add(20);
3  inc10(3); // => 13
4  inc20(3); // => 23
```

And of course, these all have their own closure scopes (closures are created at function creation time — when add() is invoked), so the original inc() keeps working:

```
1  inc(3) // 4
```

When we create inc() with the function call add(1), the a parameter inside add() gets *fixed* to 1 inside the returned function that gets assigned to inc.

Then when we call inc(3), the b parameter inside add() is replaced with the argument value, 3, and the application completes, returning the sum of 1 and 3.

All curried functions are a form of higher-order function which allows you to create specialized versions of the original function for the specific use case at hand.

Why do we curry?

Curried functions are particularly useful in the context of **function composition**.

In algebra, given two functions, g and f:

$$g : a \to b f : b \to c$$

You can compose those functions together to create a new function, h from a directly to c:

$$h : a \to c h : f \circ g h(x) = f(g(x))$$

In JavaScript:

```
1  const g = n => n + 1;
2  const f = n => n * 2;
3
4  const h = x => f(g(x));
5
6  h(20); //=> 42
```

The algebra definition:

$$(f \circ g)(x) = f(g(x))$$

Can be translated into JavaScript:

```
1  const compose = (f, g) => x => f(g(x));
```

But that would only be able to compose two functions at a time. In algebra, it's possible to write:

$$f \circ g \circ h$$

We can write a function to compose as many functions as you like. In other words, compose() creates a pipeline of functions with the output of one function connected to the input of the next.

Here's the way I usually write it:

```
1  // compose = (...fns) => x => y
2  const compose = (...fns) => x => fns.reduceRight((y, f) => f(y), x);
```

This version takes any number of functions and returns a function which takes the initial value, and then uses reduceRight() to iterate right-to-left over each function, f, in fns, and apply it in turn to the accumulated value, y. What we're accumulating with the accumulator, y in this function is the return value for the function returned by compose().

Now we can write our composition like this:

```
1  const g = n => n + 1;
2  const f = n => n * 2;
3
4  // replace `x => f(g(x))` with `compose(f, g)`
5  const h = compose(f, g);
6
7  h(20); //=> 42
```

Trace

Function composition using point-free style creates very concise, readable code, but it can come at the cost of easy debugging. What if you want to inspect the values between functions? `trace()` is a handy utility that will allow you to do just that. It takes the form of a curried function:

```javascript
const trace = label => value => {
  console.log(`${ label }: ${ value }`);
  return value;
};
```

Now we can inspect the pipeline:

```javascript
const compose = (...fns) => x => fns.reduceRight((y, f) => f(y), x);

const trace = label => value => {
  console.log(`${ label }: ${ value }`);
  return value;
};

const g = n => n + 1;
const f = n => n * 2;

/*
Note: function application order is
bottom-to-top:
*/
const h = compose(
  trace('after f'),
  f,
  trace('after g'),
  g
);

h(20);
/*
after g: 21
after f: 42
*/
```

`compose()` is a great utility, but when we need to compose more than two functions, it's sometimes handy if we can read them in top-to-bottom order. We can do that by reversing the order the functions are called. There's another composition utility called `pipe()` that composes in reverse order:

```
const pipe = (...fns) => x => fns.reduce((y, f) => f(y), x);
```

Now we can write the above code like this:

```
const pipe = (...fns) => x => fns.reduce((y, f) => f(y), x);

const trace = label => value => {
  console.log(`${ label }: ${ value }`);
  return value;
};

const g = n => n + 1;
const f = n => n * 2;

/*
Now the function application order
runs top-to-bottom:
*/
const h = pipe(
  g,
  trace('after g'),
  f,
  trace('after f'),
);

h(20);
/*
after g: 21
after f: 42
*/
```

Curry and Function Composition, Together

Even outside the context of function composition, currying is certainly a useful abstraction we can use to specialize functions. For example, a curried version of `map()` can be specialized to do many different things:

```
 1  const map = fn => mappable => mappable.map(fn);
 2
 3  const pipe = (...fns) => x => fns.reduce((y, f) => f(y), x);
 4  const log = (...args) => console.log(...args);
 5
 6  const arr = [1, 2, 3, 4];
 7  const isEven = n => n % 2 === 0;
 8
 9  const stripe = n => isEven(n) ? 'dark' : 'light';
10  const stripeAll = map(stripe);
11  const striped = stripeAll(arr);
12  log(striped);
13  // => ["light", "dark", "light", "dark"]
14
15  const double = n => n * 2;
16  const doubleAll = map(double);
17  const doubled = doubleAll(arr);
18  log(doubled);
19  // => [2, 4, 6, 8]
```

But the real power of curried functions is that they simplify function composition. A function can take any number of inputs, but can only return a single output. In order for functions to be composable, the output type must align with the expected input type:

```
 1  f: a => b
 2  g:    b => c
 3  h: a     =>    c
```

If the g function above expected two parameters, the output from f wouldn't line up with the input for g:

```
 1  f: a => b
 2  g:    (x, b) => c
 3  h: a     =>    c
```

How do we get x into g in this scenario? Usually, the answer is to *curry g*.

Remember the definition of a curried function is a function which takes multiple parameters *one at a time* by taking the first argument and returning a series of functions which each take the next argument until all the parameters have been collected.

The key words in that definition are "one at a time". The reason that curried functions are so convenient for function composition is that they transform functions which expect multiple parameters into functions which can take a single argument, allowing them to fit in a function composition pipeline. Take the trace() function as an example, from earlier:

```javascript
const pipe = (...fns) => x => fns.reduce((y, f) => f(y), x);

const trace = label => value => {
  console.log(`${ label }: ${ value }`);
  return value;
};

const g = n => n + 1;
const f = n => n * 2;

const h = pipe(
  g,
  trace('after g'),
  f,
  trace('after f'),
);

h(20);
/*
after g: 21
after f: 42
*/
```

trace() defines two parameters, but takes them one at a time, allowing us to specialize the function inline. If trace() were not curried, we couldn't use it in this way. We'd have to write the pipeline like this:

```javascript
const pipe = (...fns) => x => fns.reduce((y, f) => f(y), x);

const trace = (label, value) => {
  console.log(`${ label }: ${ value }`);
  return value;
};

const g = n => n + 1;
const f = n => n * 2;

const h = pipe(
  g,
  // the trace() calls are no longer point-free,
  // introducing the intermediary variable, `x`.
  x => trace('after g', x),
  f,
```

```
17    x => trace('after f', x),
18  );
19
20  h(20);
```

But simply currying a function is not enough. You also need to ensure that the function is expecting parameters in the correct order to specialize them. Look what happens if we curry `trace()` again, but flip the parameter order:

```
1   const pipe = (...fns) => x => fns.reduce((y, f) => f(y), x);
2
3   const trace = value => label => {
4     console.log(`${ label }: ${ value }`);
5     return value;
6   };
7
8   const g = n => n + 1;
9   const f = n => n * 2;
10
11  const h = pipe(
12    g,
13    // the trace() calls can't be point-free,
14    // because arguments are expected in the wrong order.
15    x => trace(x)('after g'),
16    f,
17    x => trace(x)('after f'),
18  );
19
20  h(20);
```

If you're in a pinch, you can fix that problem with a function called `flip()`, which simply flips the order of two parameters:

```
1   const flip = fn => a => b => fn(b)(a);
```

Now we can crate a `flippedTrace()` function:

```
1   const flippedTrace = flip(trace);
```

And use it like this:

```javascript
const flip = fn => a => b => fn(b)(a);
const pipe = (...fns) => x => fns.reduce((y, f) => f(y), x);

const trace = value => label => {
  console.log(`${ label }: ${ value }`);
  return value;
};
const flippedTrace = flip(trace);

const g = n => n + 1;
const f = n => n * 2;

const h = pipe(
  g,
  flippedTrace('after g'),
  f,
  flippedTrace('after f'),
);

h(20);
```

But a better approach is to write the function correctly in the first place. The style is sometimes called "data last", which means that you should take the specializing parameters first, and take the data the function will act on last. That gives us the original form of the function:

```javascript
const trace = label => value => {
  console.log(`${ label }: ${ value }`);
  return value;
};
```

Each application of trace() to a label creates a specialized version of the trace function that is used in the pipeline, where the label is fixed inside the returned partial application of trace. So this:

```javascript
const trace = label => value => {
  console.log(`${ label }: ${ value }`);
  return value;
};

const traceAfterG = trace('after g');
```

... is equivalent to this:

```
1  const traceAfterG = value => {
2    const label = 'after g';
3    console.log(`${ label }: ${ value }`);
4    return value;
5  };
```

If we swapped `trace('after g')` for `traceAfterG`, it would mean the same thing:

```
1  const pipe = (...fns) => x => fns.reduce((y, f) => f(y), x);
2
3  const trace = label => value => {
4    console.log(`${ label }: ${ value }`);
5    return value;
6  };
7
8  // The curried version of trace()
9  // saves us from writing all this code...
10 const traceAfterG = value => {
11   const label = 'after g';
12   console.log(`${ label }: ${ value }`);
13   return value;
14 };
15
16 const g = n => n + 1;
17 const f = n => n * 2;
18
19 const h = pipe(
20   g,
21   traceAfterG,
22   f,
23   trace('after f'),
24 );
25
26 h(20);
```

Conclusion

A **curried function** is a function which takes multiple parameters one at a time, by taking the first argument, and returning a series of functions which each take the next argument until all the parameters have been fixed, and the function application can complete, at which point, the resulting value is returned.

A **partial application** is a function which has already been applied to some — but not yet all — of its arguments. The arguments which the function has already been applied to are called *fixed parameters*.

Point-free style is a way of defining a function without reference to its arguments. Generally, a point-free function is created by calling a function which returns a function, such as a curried function.

Curried functions are great for function composition, because they allow you to easily convert an n-ary function into the unary function form needed for function composition pipelines: Functions in a pipeline must expect exactly one argument.

Data last functions are convenient for function composition, because they can be easily used in point-free style.

Abstraction & Composition

The more I mature in software development, the more I value the fundamentals — insights that seemed trivial when I was a beginner, but now hold profound significance with the benefit of experience.

> "In the martial art of Karate [...] the symbol of pride for a black belt is to wear it long enough such that the dye fades to white as to symbolize returning to the beginner state."
> ~ John Maeda, "The Laws of Simplicity: Design, Technology, Business, Life"[33]

Abstraction is "the process of considering something independently of its associations, attributes, or concrete accompaniments," according to Google dictionary.

The word abstraction comes from the latin verb *abstrahere*, which means "to draw away". I like this insight. Abstraction is about removing things – but what are we removing, and to what end?

Sometimes I like to translate words into other languages and then translate them back to English to get a sense of other associations we don't commonly think about in English. When I translate "abstraction" into Yiddish and back, the result is "absentminded". I like this, too. An absentminded person is running on autopilot, not actively thinking about what they're doing... just doing it.

Abstraction lets us run on autopilot, safely. All software is automation. Given enough time, anything you do on a computer, you could do with paper, ink, and carrier pigeons. Software just takes care of all the little details that would be too time consuming to do manually.

All software is abstraction, hiding away all the hard work and mindless details while we reap the benefits.

A lot of software processes get repeated again and again. If, during the problem decomposition stage, we decided to reimplement the repeated stuff over and over again, that would require a lot of unnecessary work. It would be silly at the very least. In many cases, it would be impractical.

Instead, we remove duplication by writing a component of some kind (a function, module, class, etc...), giving it a name (identity), and reusing it as many times as we like.

The process of decomposition is the process of abstraction. Successful abstraction implies that the result is a set of independently useful and recomposable components. From this we get an important principle of software architecture:

Software solutions should be decomposable into their component parts, and recomposable into new solutions, without changing the internal component implementation details.

---

[33]https://www.amazon.com/Laws-Simplicity-Design-Technology-Business/dp/0262134721/ref=as_li_ss_tl?ie=UTF8&qid=1516330765&sr=8-1&keywords=the+laws+of+simplicity&linkCode=ll1&tag=eejs-20&linkId=287b1d3357fa799ce7563584e098c5d8

Abstraction is simplification.

> "Simplicity is about subtracting the obvious and adding the meaningful." ~ John Maeda, "The Laws of Simplicity: Design, Technology, Business, Life"[34]

The process of abstraction has two main components:

Generalization is the process of finding *similarities* (the obvious) in repeated patterns, and hiding the similarities behind an abstraction.

Specialization is the process of using the abstraction, supplying *only what is different* (the meaningful) for each use case.

Abstraction is the process of extracting the underlying essence of a concept. By exploring common ground between different problems from different domains, we learn how to step outside our headspace for a moment and see a problem from a different perspective. When we see the essence of a problem, we find that a good solution may apply to many other problems. If we code the solution well, we can radically reduce the complexity of our application.

> "If you touch one thing with deep awareness, you touch everything." ~ Thich Nhat Hanh

This principle can be used to radically reduce the code required to build an application.

Abstraction in Software

Abstraction in software takes many forms:

- Algorithms
- Data structures
- Modules
- Classes
- Frameworks

And my personal favorite:

> "Sometimes, the elegant implementation is just a function. Not a method. Not a class. Not a framework. Just a function." ~ John Carmack (Id Software, Oculus VR)

Functions make great abstractions because they possess the properties that are essential for a good abstraction:

- Identity - The ability to assign a name to it and reuse it in different contexts.
- Composable - The ability to compose simple functions to form more complex functions.

---

[34]https://www.amazon.com/Laws-Simplicity-Design-Technology-Business/dp/0262134721/ref=as_li_ss_tl?ie=UTF8&qid=1516330765&sr=8-1&keywords=the+laws+of+simplicity&linkCode=ll1&tag=eejs-20&linkId=287b1d3357fa799ce7563584e098c5d8

Abstraction through composition

The most useful functions for abstraction in software are *pure functions*, which share modular characteristics with functions from math. In math, a function given the same inputs will always return the same output. It's possible to see functions as relations between inputs and outputs. Given some input A, a function f will produce B as output. You could say that f defines a relationship between A and B:

$$f : A \to B$$

Likewise, we could define another function, g, which defines a relationship between B and C:

$$g : B \to C$$

This *implies* another function h which defines a relationship directly from A to C:

$$h : A \to C$$

Those relationships form the structure of the problem space, and the way you compose functions in your application forms the structure of your application.

Good abstractions simplify by hiding structure, the same way h reduces $A \to B \to C$ down to $A \to C$.

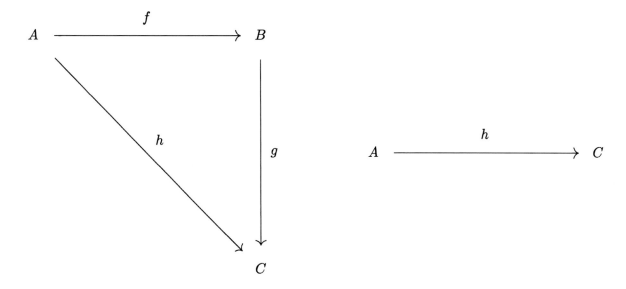

Function composition diagram

How to Do More with Less Code

Abstraction is the key to doing more with less code. For example, imagine you have a function which simply adds two numbers:

```
const add = (a, b) => a + b;
```

But you use it frequently to increment, it might make sense to **fix** one of those numbers:

```
const a = add(1, 1);
const b = add(a, 1);
const c = add(b, 1);
// ...
```

We can **curry** the add function:

```
const add = a => b => a + b;
```

And then create a **partial application**, applying the function to its first argument, and returning a new function that takes the next argument:

```
const inc = add(1);
```

Now we can use `inc` instead of `add` when we need to increment by 1, which reduces the code required:

```
const a = inc(1);
const b = inc(a);
const c = inc(b);
// ...
```

In this case, `inc` is just a *specialized* version of add. All curried functions are abstractions. In fact, all higher-order functions are generalizations that you can specialize by passing one or more arguments.

For example, `Array.prototype.map()` is a higher-order function that abstracts the idea of applying a function to each element of an array in order to return a new array of processed values. We can write map as a curried function to make this more obvious:

```
const map = f => arr => arr.map(f);
```

This version of `map` takes the specializing function and then returns a specialized version of itself that takes the array to be processed:

```
const f = n => n * 2;

const doubleAll = map(f);
const doubled = doubleAll([1, 2, 3]);
// => [2, 4, 6]
```

Note that the definition of `doubleAll` required a trivial amount of code: `map(f)` — that's it! That's the entire definition. Starting with useful abstractions as our building blocks, we can construct fairly complex behavior with very little new code.

Conclusion

Most software developers spend their entire careers creating and composing abstractions without a good fundamental grasp of abstraction or composition.

When you create abstractions, you should be deliberate about it, and you should be aware of the good abstractions that have already been made available to you (such as the always useful `map`, `filter`, and `reduce`). Learn to recognize characteristics of good abstractions:

- Composable
- Reusable
- Independent
- Concise
- Simple

Reduce

Reduce (aka: fold, accumulate) utility commonly used in functional programming that lets you iterate over a list, applying a function to an accumulated value and the next item in the list, until the iteration is complete and the accumulated value gets returned. Many useful things can be implemented with reduce. Frequently, it's the most elegant way to do any non-trivial processing on a collection of items.

Reduce takes a reducer function and an initial value, and returns the accumulated value. For `Array.prototype.reduce()`, the initial list is provided by `this`, so it's not one of the arguments:

```
array.reduce(
  reducer: (accumulator: Any, current: Any) => Any,
  initialValue: Any
) => accumulator: Any
```

Let's sum an array:

```
1  [2, 4, 6].reduce((acc, n) => acc + n, 0); // 12
```

For each element in the array, the reducer is called and passed the accumulator and the current value. The reducer's job is to "fold" the current value into the accumulated value somehow. How is not specified, and specifying how is the purpose of the reducer function. The reducer returns the new accumulated value, and `reduce()` moves on to the next value in the array. The reducer may need an initial value to start with, so most implementations take an initial value as a parameter.

In the case of this summing reducer, the first time the reducer is called, `acc` starts at `0` (the value we passed to `.reduce()` as the second parameter). The reducer returns `0 + 2` (2 was the first element in the array), which is 2. For the next call, `acc = 2`, `n = 4` and the reducer returns the result of `2 + 4` (6). In the last iteration, `acc = 6`, `n = 6`, and the reducer returns 12. Since the iteration is finished, `.reduce()` returns the final accumulated value, 12.

In this case, we passed in an anonymous reducing function, but we can abstract it and give it a name:

```
1  const summingReducer = (acc, n) => acc + n;
2  [2, 4, 6].reduce(summingReducer, 0); // 12
```

Normally, `reduce()` works left to right. In JavaScript, we also have `[].reduceRight()`, which works right to left. In other words, if you applied `.reduceRight()` to `[2, 4, 6]`, the first iteration would use 6 as the first value for `n`, and it would work its way back and finish with 2.

Reduce is Versatile

Reduce is versatile. It's easy to define `map()`, `filter()`, `forEach()` and lots of other interesting things using reduce:

Map:

```
1  const map = (fn, arr) => arr.reduce((acc, item, index, arr) => {
2    return acc.concat(fn(item, index, arr));
3  }, []);
```

For map, our accumulated value is a new array with a new element for each value in the original array. The new values are generated by applying the passed in mapping function (`fn`) to each element in the `arr` argument. We accumulate the new array by calling `fn` with the current element, and concatenating the result to the accumulator array, `acc`.

Filter:

```
1  const filter = (fn, arr) => arr.reduce((newArr, item) => {
2    return fn(item) ? newArr.concat([item]) : newArr;
3  }, []);
```

Filter works in much the same way as map, except that we take a predicate function and *conditionally* append the current value to the new array if the element passes the predicate check (`fn(item)` returns true).

For each of the above examples, you have a list of data, iterate over that data applying some function and folding the results into an accumulated value. Lots of applications spring to mind. But what if *your data is a list of functions?*

Compose:

Reduce is also a convenient way to compose functions. Remember function composition: If you want to apply the function f to the result of g of x i.e., the composition, f . g, you could use the following JavaScript:

```
1  f(g(x))
```

Reduce lets us abstract that process to work on any number of functions, so you could easily define a function that would represent:

```
1  f(g(h(x)))
```

To make that happen, we'll need to run reduce in reverse. That is, right-to-left, rather than left-to-right. Thankfully, JavaScript provides a `.reduceRight()` method:

```
1  const compose = (...fns) => x => fns.reduceRight((v, f) => f(v), x);
```

> Note: If JavaScript had not provided `[].reduceRight()`, you could still implement `reduceRight()` – using `reduce()`. I'll leave it to adventurous readers to figure out how.

Pipe:

`compose()` is great if you want to represent the composition from the inside-out – that is, in the math notation sense. But what if you want to think of it as a sequence of events?

Imagine we want to add 1 to a number and then double it. With 'compose(), that would be:

```
const add1 = n => n + 1;
const double = n => n * 2;

const add1ThenDouble = compose(
  double,
  add1
);

add1ThenDouble(2); // 6
// ((2 + 1 = 3) * 2 = 6)
```

See the problem? The first step is listed last, so in order to understand the sequence, you'll need to start at the bottom of the list and work your way backwards to the top.

Or we can reduce left-to-right as you normally would, instead of right-to-left:

```
const pipe = (...fns) => x => fns.reduce((v, f) => f(v), x);
```

Now you can write add1ThenDouble() like this:

```
const add1ThenDouble = pipe(
  add1,
  double
);

add1ThenDouble(2); // 6
// ((2 + 1 = 3) * 2 = 6)
```

This is important because sometimes if you compose backwards, you get a different result:

```
const doubleThenAdd1 = pipe(
  double,
  add1
);

doubleThenAdd1(2); // 5
```

We'll go into more details on compose() and pipe() later. What you should understand right now is that reduce() is a very powerful tool, and you really need to learn it. Just be aware that if you get very tricky with reduce, some people may have a hard time following along.

A Word on Redux

You may have heard the term "reducer" used to describe the important state update bits of Redux. As of this writing, Redux is the most popular state management library/architecture for web applications built using React and Angular (the latter via `ngrx/store`).

Redux uses reducer functions to manage application state. A Redux-style reducer takes the current state and an action object and returns the new state:

```
reducer(state: Any, action: { type: String, payload: Any}) => newState: Any
```

Redux has some reducer rules you need to keep in mind:

1. A reducer called with no parameters should return its valid initial state.
2. If the reducer isn't going to handle the action type, it still needs to return the state.
3. Redux reducers **must be pure functions**.

Let's rewrite our summing reducer as a Redux-style reducer that reduces over action objects:

```
const ADD_VALUE = 'ADD_VALUE';

const summingReducer = (state = 0, action = {}) => {
  const { type, payload } = action;

  switch (type) {
    case ADD_VALUE:
      return state + payload.value;
    default: return state;
  }
};
```

The cool thing about Redux is that the reducers are just standard reducers that you can plug into any `reduce()` implementation which respects the reducer function signature, including `[].reduce()`. That means you can create an array of action objects and reduce over them to get a snapshot of state representing the same state you'd have if those same actions were dispatched to your store:

```
1  const actions = [
2    { type: 'ADD_VALUE', payload: { value: 1 } },
3    { type: 'ADD_VALUE', payload: { value: 1 } },
4    { type: 'ADD_VALUE', payload: { value: 1 } },
5  ];
6
7  actions.reduce(summingReducer, 0); // 3
```

That makes unit testing Redux-style reducers a breeze.

Conclusion

You should be starting to see that reduce is an incredibly useful and versatile abstraction. It's definitely a little trickier to understand than map or filter, but it is an essential tool in your functional programming utility belt – one you can use to make a lot of other great tools.

Functors & Categories

A **functor data type** is something you can map over. It's a container which has a map operation which can be used to apply a function to the values inside it. When you see a functor datatype, you should think *"mappable"*. In JavaScript, functor types are typically represented as an object with a `.map()` method that maps from inputs to outputs, e.g., `Array.prototype.map()`. A common analogy is to think of a functor data structure as a box, and map as a way to apply a function to each item contained inside the box, which creates a new box containing the outputs.

$$[Box\ of\ a's] \xrightarrow{map(a \to b)} [Box\ of\ b's]$$

In category theory, a **functor** is a structure preserving map from category to category, where "structure preserving" means that the relationships between objects and morphisms are retained. All functor map operations must obey two axioms, called "the functor laws". We'll get to category theory and the related math later. You don't need to understand it, yet.

The JavaScript array `.map()` method is a good example of a functor, but many other kinds of objects can be mapped over as well, including promises, streams, trees, objects, etc.

JavaScript's built in array and promise objects act like functors. For collections (arrays, streams, trees, etc.), `.map()` typically iterates over the collection and applies the given function to each value in the collection, but not all functors iterate. The point of a functor is to apply a given function to values contained within the context of the structure.

Promises use `.then()` instead of `.map()`. You can usually think of `.then()` as an asynchronous `.map()` method, except when you have a nested promise, in which case it automatically unwraps the outer promise. Again, for values which are not promises, `.then()` acts like an asynchronous `.map()`. For values which are promises themselves, `.then()` acts like the `.flatMap()` method from monads (sometimes also called `.chain()` or `.bind()`). So, promises are not quite functors, and not quite monads, but in practice, you can usually treat them as either. We'll get to monads later.

In Haskell, the functor map operation is called `fmap` and has the signature:

```
1  fmap :: (a -> b) -> f a -> f b
```

Given a function that takes an `a` and returns a `b` and a box with zero or more `a`s inside it: `fmap` returns a box with zero or more `b`s inside it. The `f a` and `f b` bits can be read as "a functor of `a`" and "a functor of `b`", meaning `f a` has `a`s inside the box, and `f b` has `b`s inside the box.

In JavaScript, it's common to pair the data type with methods that act on the data type. In other words, the value is stored with the instance context, so the signature above becomes:

```
functor.map = Functor(a) ~> (a => b) => Functor(b)
```

The squiggly arrow (~>) represents the instance being mapped over — the value that `this` points to. It's analogous to the `f a` in the Haskell signature above.

You can read the signature as `functor.map`, beginning with a functor of a, take a function from a to b, and return a functor of b.

Using a functor is easy — just call `.map()`:

```
const a = [1, 2, 3];
const b = a.map(x => x * 2);

console.log(
  b // [2, 4, 6]
);
```

Why Functors?

Functors are great for several reasons:

- The details of the underlying data structure implementation are abstracted away. Users don't need to know if iteration is required, or how it's handled if it is. You can map over arrays, streams, trees, or anything else.
- Functors hide the types of the data they contain, which allows you to act on the containers using generic functions, without caring about what you're storing inside them. You don't need special arrays for numbers, and special arrays for strings. Instead, you pass functions into `map()` that can deal with the type contained inside the functor.
- Mapping over an empty functor is the same as mapping over a functor containing many items. Switching logic is not needed in the case of an empty collection, and there's no need to keep track of iteration state if the data structure enumerates over a collection of items.
- Most importantly, functors allow you to easily compose functions over the data inside.

Imagine you're building a social network that lets you post updates and lets your friends comment. You need to wrap some UI around the comments before displaying them to the user. In addition, each comment may also have its own comments. In the following example, Bartosz Milewski posts a comment, and JS Cheerleader comments on his comment.

Comments UI

There are two ways to process the comments: **Iterate manually** with imperative code, or **map over them** with declarative code. If you chose to iterate manually, there are some disadvantages you should be aware of:

- The imperative approach is more code. The `iterateComments()` function below doesn't need to exist at all if we map, instead. More code = more surface area for bugs to hide in = more bugs.
- If the list of comments is very large, you have to wait for the entire list to arrive from the server before you can even begin to draw the comments to the screen. If you had used map, instead, you could swap out the array for a streaming data type and you wouldn't need to change the UI component at all.

```javascript
import React from "react";
import ReactDOM from "react-dom";
import getAvatar from './get-avatar';

const getComments = () => [
  {
    name: 'Bartosz Milewski',
    avatar: getAvatar('bartosz'),
    body: 'I like functors.',
    comments: [
      {
        name: 'JS Cheerleader',
        avatar: getAvatar('jsCheerleader'),
        body: 'Functors are cool!'
      }
    ]
  }
];

const iterateComments = (comments) => {
  // We have to know how to get the length here:
  const length = comments.length;
```

```
23    const children = [];
24
25    // We need conditional logic to prevent
26    // running the code if there are no comments,
27    // and to stop looping when we're done.
28    // We also need to maintain an internal
29    // index, `i`:
30    for (let i = 0; i < length; i++) {
31      // We have to know how to add to the collection
32      // here:
33      children.push(comment(comments[i]));
34    }
35
36    return children;
37  };
38
39  const comment = ({ name, avatar, body, comments = []}) => (
40    <div className="comment">
41      <img src={avatar} />
42      <span className="user-name">{ name}</span>
43      <div className="comment-body">{body}</div>
44      <div className="comments">{ iterateComments(comments) }</div>
45    </div>
46  );
47
48  function App() {
49    return (
50      <div className="App">
51        <div>{getComments().map(comment)}</div>
52      </div>
53    );
54  }
55
56  const rootElement = document.getElementById("root");
57  ReactDOM.render(<App />, rootElement);
```

Or you could just use `.map()`. In that case you can delete the entire `iterateComments()` function and replace the function call with `comments.map(comment)`:

```
 1  import React from "react";
 2  import ReactDOM from "react-dom";
 3  import getAvatar from './get-avatar';
 4
 5  const getComments = () => [
 6    {
 7      name: 'Bartosz Milewski',
 8      avatar: getAvatar('bartosz'),
 9      body: 'I like functors.',
10      comments: [
11        {
12          name: 'JS Cheerleader',
13          avatar: getAvatar('jsCheerleader'),
14          body: 'Functors are cool!'
15        }
16      ]
17    }
18  ];
19
20  const comment = ({ name, avatar, body, comments = []}) => (
21    <div className="comment">
22      <img src={avatar} />
23      <span className="user-name">{ name}</span>
24      <div className="comment-body">{body}</div>
25      <div className="comments">{ comments.map(comment) }</div>
26    </div>
27  );
28
29  function App() {
30    return (
31      <div className="App">
32        <div>{getComments().map(comment)}</div>
33      </div>
34    );
35  }
36
37  const rootElement = document.getElementById("root");
38  ReactDOM.render(<App />, rootElement);
```

Notice that there's no special logic dealing with how many times to call `comment` in the `comments` `div`. The entire logic expression is simply `comments.map(comment)`.

Functor Laws

Functors come from category theory: a branch of abstract algebra. A category is a collection of objects and arrows between objects. Objects can be anything, but it's generally useful to think of them as sets of things, like types in programming languages. Arrows are like functions which map between objects. In programming, arrows are usually represented as functions.

Categories have two important properties:

1. **Identity:** $\forall A \in C.\ id_A = 1_A : A \to A$ For all objects A in category C, there must be an identity arrow that maps back to the same object, represented as id_A or 1_A.
2. **Composition:** $\forall (A \xrightarrow{g} B \xrightarrow{f} C).\ A \xrightarrow{h:f \circ g} C$ For all pairs of arrows $g : A \to B$, $f : B \to C$, there exists an arrow $A \xrightarrow{h:f \circ g} C$.

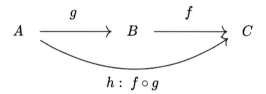

Composition: $\forall (A \xrightarrow{g} B \xrightarrow{f} C).\ A \xrightarrow{h:f \circ g} C$

A functor is a mapping between categories. Functors must respect identity and composition.

The **functor laws** are the axioms that ensure that identity and composition are respected.

Identity

$$F(a) \xrightarrow{map(id:\ a \to a)} F(a) = F(a)$$

If you pass the identity function (`x => x`) into `a.map()`, where `a` is any functor type, the result should be equivalent to `a`:

```
const a = [20];
const b = a.map(a => a);

console.log(
  a.toString() === b.toString() // true
);
```

Composition

$$F(a) \xrightarrow{map(g)} F(b) \xrightarrow{map(f)} F(c) = F(a) \xrightarrow{map(f \circ g)} F(c)$$

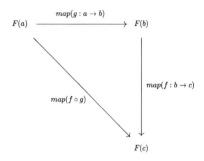

Composition law diagram

```
1   const g = n => n + 1;
2   const f = n => n * 2;
3   const mappable = [20];
4
5   const a = mappable.map(g).map(f);
6   const b = mappable.map(x => f(g(x)));
7
8   console.log(
9     a.toString() === b.toString() // true
10  );
```

Function Composition is the application of one function to the result of another: $(f \circ g)(x) = f(g(x))$. Function composition works right to left, not left to right, which is why $f \circ g$ is frequently called *f after g*.

Functors must obey the composition law: `a.map(g).map(f)` is equivalent to `a.map(x => f(g(x)))`.

Category Theory

A lot of functional programming terms come from category theory, and the essence of category theory is composition. Category theory is scary at first, but easy. Like jumping off a diving board or riding a roller coaster. Here's the foundation of category theory in a few bullet points:

- A **category** is a collection of objects and arrows between objects (where "object" can mean just about anything). Objects are like types in programming, meaning that they usually represent sets of things with one or more elements.

- Arrows are known as **morphisms**. Morphisms map between two objects A and B, connecting them with an arrow f. They're often represented in diagrams as $A \xrightarrow{f} B$.
- All objects must have identity arrows, which are arrows pointing back to the same object, e.g., $A \xrightarrow{id_A} A$. The identity arrow can also be represented as $id_A : A \to A$ or $1_A : A \to A$.
- For any group of connected objects, $A \to B \to C$, there must be a composition which goes directly from $A \to C$.
- All morphisms are equivalent to compositions, e.g., given objects A, B and an arrow f between them: $id_B \circ f = f = f \circ id_A$

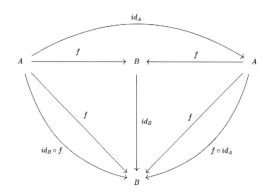

Left and right identity compositions $id_B \circ f = f = f \circ id_A$

This is analogous to function composition in code. Say you have a function of type `g: a => b`, and another function of type `f: b => c`. You could create a function `h: a => c`: `const h = x => f(g(x))`.

In category theory, the presence of $A \xrightarrow{g} B \xrightarrow{f} C$ implies that $A \xrightarrow{f \circ g} C$ also exists: $\forall (A \xrightarrow{g} B \xrightarrow{f} C)$. $A \xrightarrow{h: f \circ g} C$

Arrow composition is associative. That means that when you're composing morphisms you don't need parentheses:

$$(f \circ g) \circ h = f \circ g \circ h = f \circ (g \circ h)$$

Functor mapping is a form of function composition. In the following code, `mappable.map(g).map(f)` is equivalent to `mappable.map(x => f(g(x)))`:

```
1  const g = n => n + 1;
2  const f = n => n * 2;
3  const mappable = [20];
4
5  const a = mappable.map(g).map(f);
6  const b = mappable.map(x => f(g(x)));
7
8  console.log(
9    a.toString() === b.toString() // true
10 );
```

Build Your Own Functor

Here's a simple example of a functor:

```
1  const Identity = value => ({
2    map: fn => Identity(fn(value))
3  });
```

`Identity` takes a `value` and returns an object with a `.map()` method. The `.map()` method takes a function and returns the result of applying the function to the `value` inside the `Identity`. The returned value is wrapped inside another `Identity`. Functor maps always return an instance of the same functor type: Array on the left? Array on the right. Stream on the left? Stream on the right. Promise on the left? Promise on the right, and so on.

As you can see, `Identity` satisfies the functor laws:

```
1  // trace() is a utility to let you easily inspect
2  // the contents.
3  const trace = x => {
4    console.log(x);
5    return x;
6  };
7
8  const u = Identity(2);
9
10 // Identity law
11 const r1 = u;              // Identity(2)
12 const r2 = u.map(x => x);  // Identity(2)
13
14 r1.map(trace); // 2
```

```
15  r2.map(trace); // 2
16
17  const f = n => n + 1;
18  const g = n => n * 2;
19
20  // Composition law
21  const r3 = u.map(x => f(g(x))); // Identity(5)
22  const r4 = u.map(g).map(f);     // Identity(5)
23
24  r3.map(trace); // 5
25  r4.map(trace); // 5
```

Now you can map over any data type, just like you can map over an array. You can add the map method to any custom data type.

Curried Map

Functional programming is all about composing tiny functions to create higher level abstractions. What if you want a generic map that works with any functor? You could partially apply arguments to create new mapping functions that work with any mappable type!

```
1   // import curry from 'lodash/fp/curry';
2   // OR
3   // import curry from 'ramda/curry';
4   // OR use this magic spell:
5   const curry = (
6     f, arr = []
7   ) => (...args) => (
8     a => a.length === f.length ?
9       f(...a) :
10      curry(f, a)
11  )([...arr, ...args]);
12
13  const Identity = value => ({
14    map: fn => Identity(fn(value))
15  });
16
17  const map = curry((fn, mappable) => mappable.map(fn));
18  const log = x => console.log(x);
19
20  const double = n => n * 2;
21  const mdouble = map(double);
```

```
22
23  mdouble(Identity(4)).map(log); // 8
24  mdouble([4]).map(log);         // 8
```

Conclusion

Functors data types are things we can map over. You can think of them as containers which can have functions applied to their contents to produce a new container with the results inside.

In category theory, **a functor is a structure preserving map from category to category**, where "structure preserving" means that the relationships between objects and morphisms are retained.

A **category** is a collection of objects and arrows between objects. Arrows represent morphisms, which we can roughly think of as functions in code. Each object in a category has an identity morphism $A \xrightarrow{id_A} A$. For any chain of objects $A \xrightarrow{g} B \xrightarrow{f} C$ there exists a composition $A \xrightarrow{h:f \circ g} C$.

Functors are great higher-order abstractions that allow you compose functions over the contents of a container without coupling those functions to the structure or implementation details of the functor data type. Functors form the foundation of other very useful algebraic structures, such as monads.

Monads

"Once you understand monads, you immediately become incapable of explaining them to anyone else" Lady Monadgreen's curse ~ Gilad Bracha (used famously by Douglas Crockford)

"Dr. Hoenikker used to say that any scientist who couldn't explain to an eight-year-old what he was doing was a charlatan." ~ Kurt Vonnegut's novel Cat's Cradle

Before you begin to learn this, you should already know:

- Function composition: `compose(f, g) = f(g(x))`
- Functor basics: An understanding of the `Array.prototype.map()` operation.

If you go searching the internet for "monad" you're going to get bombarded by impenetrable category theory math and a bunch of people "helpfully" explaining monads in terms of burritos and space suits.

Monads are simple. The language used to describe them is hard. Let's cut to the essence.

A **monad** is a way of composing functions that require context in addition to the return value, such as computation, branching, or effects. Monads **map** $M(a) \xrightarrow{map(a \to b)} M(b)$ and **flatten** $M(M(a)) \xrightarrow{flatten} M(a)$, so that the types line up for type lifting functions like $a \xrightarrow{f} M(b)$, and $b \xrightarrow{g} M(c)$, making them composable.

Given two functions, $a \xrightarrow{f} M(b)$ and $b \xrightarrow{g} M(c)$, monads let us compose them to produce $h : a \xrightarrow{f \text{ then } g} M(c)$ where *then* represents the Kleisli arrow operator (`>=>` in Haskell). It's similar to the composition operator, ∘, but works in the opposite direction. You can think of it as $flatMap(g) \circ f$ (`flatMap(g)` *after* `f`). It's the monad equivalent of $g \circ f$. I use "`then`" for the Kleisli composition operator to clarify the order of operations and make the text more friendly to people who are not familiar with category theory or Haskell notation.

> **Note:** JavaScript does not have a Kleisli composition operator. Attempting to use `>=>` in JavaScript code will result in "`SyntaxError: Unexpected token >`". JavaScript *does* have a `.then()` method on the `Promise` object.

- Function composition composes functions of type `a => b`
- Functor map composes functions of type `a => b` in a functor context: `Functor(a).map(a => b)` returns `Functor(b)`.

- Monad flatMap composes functions of type `a => Monad(b)` in a monad context: `Monad(a).flatMap(a => M(b))` returns `Monad(b)`. FlatMap *maps* and *flattens* in one operation.

In other words:

- Functions can compose: `a => b => c` becomes `a => c`
- Functors can compose functions with context: given `F(a)` and two functions, `a => b => c`, return `F(c)`.
- Monads can compose type lifting functions: `a => M(b), b => M(c)` becomes `a => M(c)`

But what do "flatten" and "map" and "context" mean?

- **Map** means, "apply a function to an `a` and return a `b`". Given some input, return some output. The functor map operation does that inside the context of a container called a functor data type, which returns a new container with the results.
- **Context** is the computational detail of the monad. The functor or monad supplies some computation to be performed during the mapping process, such as iterating over a list of things, or waiting for a future value to resolve. The point of functors and monads is to abstract that context away so we don't have to worry about it while we're composing operations. Mapping inside the context means that you apply a function from `a => b` (for functors) or `a => Monad(b)` (for monads) to the values inside the context, and return new values of type `b` wrapped inside the same kind of context. Observables on the left? Observables on the right: `Observable(a) => Observable(b)`. Arrays on the left side? Arrays on the right side: `Array(a) => Array(b)`.
- **Type lift** means to lift a type into a context, wrapping values inside a data type that supplies the computational context `a => M(a)`.
- **Flatten** can be used to unwrap an extra layer of context that might be added by applying a type lifting function using a functor map operation. If you map a function of type `a => M(b)` with the functor map operation, it will return a value of type `M(M(b))`. Flatten unwraps the extra layer of context: `M(M(b)) => M(b)`. Monads are not required to directly expose a flatten operation. It happens automatically inside flatMap.
- **FlatMap** is the operation that defines a monad. It combines map and flatten into a single operation used to compose type lifting functions (`a => M(b)`).

Example of a functor context in JavaScript:

```
1  const x = 20;              // Some data of type `a`
2  const f = n => n * 2;      // A function from `a` to `b`
3  const arr = Array.of(x);   // The type lift.
4  // JS has type lift sugar for arrays: [x]
5
6  // .map() applies the function f to the value x
7  // in the context of the array.
8  const result = arr.map(f); // [40]
```

In this case, `Array` is the context, and `x` is the value we're mapping over. But what if we have a function that takes a value and returns an array of values? For example, this `echo()` function will take a value and repeat it n times:

```
1  const echo = n => x => Array.from({ length: n }).fill(x);
```

Using `map()` with this, we'll end up with an array of arrays:

```
1  const echo = n => x => Array.from({ length: n }).fill(x);
2
3  console.log(
4    [1, 2, 3].map( echo(3) )
5    // [[1, 1, 1], [2, 2, 2], [3, 3, 3]]
6  );
```

That's fine if that's what you're looking for, but what if you want an array of numbers instead of an array of arrays of numbers? FlatMap to the rescue!

```
1  const echo = n => x => Array.from({ length: n }).fill(x);
2
3  console.log(
4    [1, 2, 3].flatMap(echo(3))
5    // => [1, 1, 1, 2, 2, 2, 3, 3, 3]
6  );
```

You're probably already using monads.

Regardless of your skill level or understanding of category theory, using monads makes your code easier to work with. Failing to take advantage of monads may make your code harder to work with (e.g., callback hell, nested conditional branches, and potentially a lot more code).

Remember, the essence of software development is composition, and monads make composition easier. Take another look at the essence of what monads are:

- Functions can compose: a => b => c becomes a => c
- Functors can compose functions with context: given F(a) and two functions, a => b => c, return F(c).
- Monads can compose type lifting functions: a => M(b), b => M(c) becomes a => M(c)

The whole reason functions exist is so you can compose them. Functions help you break down complex problems into simple problems that are easier to solve in isolation, so that you can compose them in various ways to form your application.

The key to understanding functions and their proper use is a deeper understanding of function composition.

Function composition creates pipelines that your data flows through. You put some input in the first stage of the pipeline, and some data pops out of the last stage of the pipeline, transformed. But for that to work, each stage of the pipeline must be expecting the data type that the previous stage returns.

Composing simple functions is easy, because the types all line up easily. Just match output type b to input type b and you're in business:

```
1  g: a => b
2  f:      b => c
3  h: a      => c
```

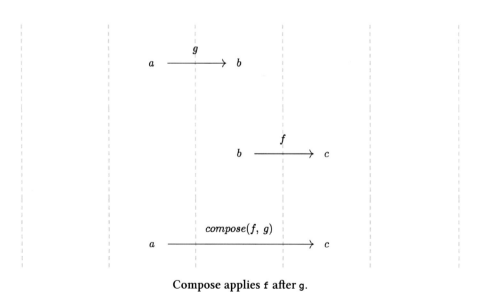

Compose applies f after g.

Composing with functors is also easy if you're mapping F(a) => F(b) because the types line up:

```
1  f: F(a) => F(b)
2  g:       F(b) => F(c)
3  h: F(a)       =>      F(c)
```

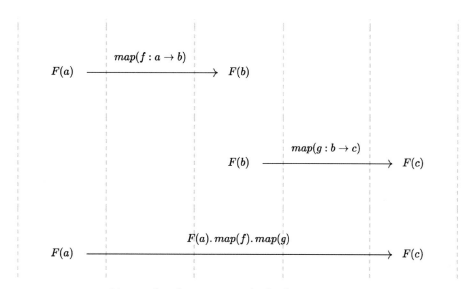

Map applies functions inside the functor context.

But if you want to compose functions from a => F(b), b => F(c), and so on, you need monads. Let's swap the F() for M() to make that clear:

```
1  f: a => M(b)
2  g:    ???   b => M(c)
3  h: a    =>     M(c)
```

Oops. In this example, *the component function types don't line up!* For g's input, we wanted type b, but what we got was type M(b) (a monad of b). Because of that misalignment, h needs to apply g in the context of M(b) because g is expecting type b, not type M(b). We can't simply f(a).map(g) like we would with a functor, because map adds a layer of extra wrapping around its return values, which would produce M(M(c)) instead of the M(c) we're expecting. We need flatMap instead of map. Monads make the types line up for lifting functions a => M(b), so that you can compose them.

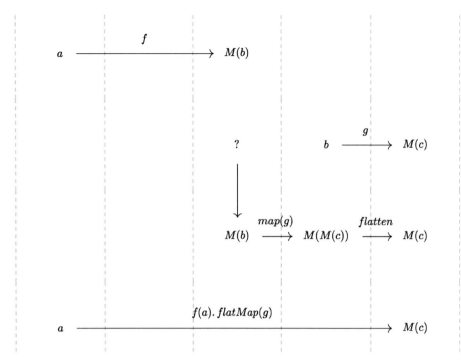

FlatMap maps and flattens in one operation.

In the above diagram, the map from `b => M(M(c))` and `flatten` from `M(M(c)) => c` happens inside the `flatMap` from `a => M(c)`. Using the `flatMap` operation, we can compose monad-returning functions with the same kinds of declarative tools we use to compose normal functions. For example, if you want to compose promise-returning functions, you can swap `pipe` for `asyncPipe` and everything else stays the same.

Monads are needed because lots of functions aren't simple mappings from `a => b`. Some functions need to deal with side effects (promises, streams), handle branching (Maybe), deal with exceptions (Either), etc...

Here's a more concrete example. What if you need to fetch a user from an asynchronous API, and then pass that user data to another asynchronous API to perform some calculation?:

```
getUserById(id: String) => Promise(User)
hasPermision(User) => Promise(Boolean)
```

Let's write some functions to demonstrate the problem. First, the utilities, `compose()` and `trace()`:

```
1  const compose = (...fns) => x => fns.reduceRight((y, f) => f(y), x);
2
3  const trace = label => value => {
4    console.log(`${ label }: ${ value }`);
5    return value;
6  };
```

Then some functions to compose:

```
1  {
2    const label = 'API call composition';
3
4    // a => Promise(b)
5    const getUserById = id => id === 3 ?
6      Promise.resolve({ name: 'Kurt', role: 'Author' }) :
7      undefined
8    ;
9
10   // b => Promise(c)
11   const hasPermission = ({ role }) => (
12     Promise.resolve(role === 'Author')
13   );
14
15   // Try to compose them. Warning: this will fail.
16   const authUser = compose(hasPermission, getUserById);
17
18   // Oops! Always false!
19   authUser(3).then(trace(label));
20  }
```

When we try to compose `hasPermission()` with `getUserById()` to form `authUser()` we run into a big problem because `hasPermission()` is expecting a `User` object and getting a `Promise(User)` instead. To fix this, we need to swap out `compose()` for `composePromises()` — a special version of compose that knows it needs to use `.then()` to accomplish the function composition:

```javascript
{
  const composeM = flatMap => (...ms) => (
    ms.reduce((f, g) => x => g(x)[flatMap](f))
  );

  const composePromises = composeM('then');

  const label = 'API call composition';

  // a => Promise(b)
  const getUserById = id => id === 3 ?
    Promise.resolve({ name: 'Kurt', role: 'Author' }) :
    undefined
  ;

  // b => Promise(c)
  const hasPermission = ({ role }) => (
    Promise.resolve(role === 'Author')
  );

  // Compose the functions (this works!)
  const authUser = composePromises(hasPermission, getUserById);

  authUser(3).then(trace(label)); // true
}
```

We'll get into what `composeM()` is doing, later.

Remember the essence of monads:

- Functions can compose: `a => b => c` becomes `a => c`
- Functors can compose functions with context: given `F(a)` and two functions, `a => b => c`, return `F(c)`.
- Monads can compose type lifting functions: `a => M(b)`, `b => M(c)` becomes `a => M(c)`

In this case, our monads are really promises, so when we compose these promise-returning functions, we have a `Promise(User)` instead of the `User` that `hasPermission()` is expecting.

What Monads are Made of

A monad is based on a simple symmetry:

- **of**: A type lift `a => M(a)`
- **map**: The application of a function `a => M(b)` inside the monad context, which yields `M(M(b))`
- **flatten**: The unwrapping of one layer of monadic context: `M(M(b)) => M(b)`

Combine `map` with `flatten`, and you get `flatMap` — function composition for monad-lifting functions, aka Kleisli composition, named after Heinrich Kleisli[35]:

- **FlatMap** Map + flatten: `f(a).flatMap(g) = M(c)`

For monads, `.map()` and `.flatten()` methods are often omitted from the public API, and instead are part of the flatMap operation. Lift + flatten don't explicitly spell out `.map()`, but you have all the ingredients you need to make it. If you can lift (`of`) and flatMap (aka chain/bind/then), you can make `.map()`:

```
const Monad = value => ({
  flatMap: f => f(value),
  map (f) {
    return this.flatMap(a => Monad.of(f(a)));
  }
});
Monad.of = x => Monad(x);

Monad(21).map(x => x * 2).map(x => console.log(x))
```

So, if you define `.of()` and `.flatMap()` for your monad, you can infer the definition of `.map()`.

The lift is the factory/constructor and/or `constructor.of()` method. In category theory, it's called "unit". All it does is lift the type into the context of the monad. It turns an `a` into a `Monad` of `a`.

In Haskell, it's called `return`, which can be awkward when you try to talk about it out-loud because nearly everyone confuses it with function returns. I almost always call it "lift" or "type lift" in prose, and `.of()` in code.

The flattening process (without the map in `.flatMap()`) is usually called `flatten()` or `join()`. Frequently (but not always), `flatten()`/`join()` is omitted completely because it's built into `.flatMap()`. Flattening is often associated with composition, so it's frequently combined with mapping. Remember, unwrapping + map are both needed to compose `a => M(a)` functions.

Depending on what kind of monad you're dealing with, the unwrapping process could be extremely simple. In the case of the identity monad, `.flatMap()` is just like `.map()`, except that you don't lift the resulting value back into the monad context. That has the effect of discarding one layer of wrapping:

---

[35]https://en.wikipedia.org/wiki/Heinrich_Kleisli

```javascript
{ // Identity monad
const Id = value => ({
  // Functor mapping
  // Preserve the wrapping for .map() by
  // passing the mapped value into the type
  // lift:
  map: f => Id.of(f(value)),

  // Monad flatMap
  // Discard one level of wrapping
  // by omitting the .of() type lift:
  flatMap: f => f(value),

  // Just a convenient way to inspect
  // the values:
  toString: () => `Id(${ value })`
});

// The type lift for this monad is just
// a reference to the factory.
Id.of = Id;
```

But the unwrapping part is also where the weird stuff like side effects, error branching, or waiting for async I/O typically hides. In all software development, composition is where all the real interesting stuff happens.

For example, with promises, `.flatMap()` is called `.then()`. Calling `promise.then(f)` won't invoke `f()` right away. Instead, it will wait for the promise to resolve, and *then* call `f()` (hence the name).

Example:

```javascript
{
  const x = 20;                      // The value
  const p = Promise.resolve(x);      // The context
  const f = n =>
    Promise.resolve(n * 2);          // The function

  const result = p.then(f);          // The application

  result.then(
    r => console.log(r)              // 40
  );
}
```

With promises, `.then()` is used instead of `.flatMap()`, but it's *almost* the same thing.

You may have heard that a promise is not strictly a monad. That's because it will only unwrap the outer promise if the value is a promise to begin with. Otherwise, `.then()` behaves like `.map()`.

But because it behaves differently for promise values and other values, `.then()` does not strictly obey all the mathematical laws that all functors and/or monads must satisfy for all given values. In practice, as long as you're aware of that behavior branching, you can usually treat them as either.

Building a Kleisli Composition Function

Let's a take deeper look at the `composeM` function we used to compose promise-lifting functions:

```
const composeM = method => (...ms) => (
  ms.reduce((f, g) => x => g(x)[method](f))
);
```

Hidden in that weird reducer is the algebraic definition of function composition: `f(g(x))`. Let's make it easier to spot:

```
{
  // The algebraic definition of function composition:
  // (f . g)(x) = f(g(x))
  const compose = (f, g) => x => f(g(x));

  const x = 20;    // The value
  const arr = [x]; // The container

  // Some functions to compose
  const g = n => n + 1;
  const f = n => n * 2;

  // Proof that .map() accomplishes function composition.
  // Chaining calls to map is function composition.
  trace('map composes')([
    arr.map(g).map(f),
    arr.map(compose(f, g))
  ]);
  // => [42], [42]
}
```

What this means is that we could write a generalized compose utility that should work for all functors which supply a `.map()` method (e.g., arrays):

```
const composeMap = (...ms) => (
  ms.reduce((f, g) => x => g(x).map(f))
);
```

This is just a slight reformulation of the standard `f(g(x))`. Given any number of functions of type `a -> Functor(b)`, iterate through each function and apply each one to its input value, `x`. The `.reduce()` method takes a function with two input values: An accumulator (`f` in this case), and the current item in the array (`g`).

We return a new function `x => g(x).map(f)` which becomes `f` in the next application. We've already proved above that `x => g(x).map(f)` is equivalent to lifting `compose(f, g)(x)` into the context of the functor. In other words, it's equivalent to applying `f(g(x))` to the values in the container: In this case, that would apply the composition to the values inside the array.

> **Performance Warning**: I'm not recommending this for arrays. Composing functions in this way would require multiple iterations over the entire array (which could contain hundreds of thousands of items). For maps over an array, compose simple `a -> b` functions first, then map over the array *once*, or optimize iterations with `.reduce()` or a transducer.

For synchronous, eager function applications over array data, this is overkill. However, lots of things are asynchronous or lazy, and lots of functions need to handle messy things like branching for exceptions or empty values.

That's where monads come in. Monads can rely on values that depend on previous asynchronous or branching actions in the composition chain. In those cases, you can't get a simple value out for simple function compositions. Your monad-returning actions take the form `a => Monad(b)` instead of `a => b`.

Whenever you have a function that takes some data, hits an API, and returns a corresponding value, and another function that takes that data, hits another API, and returns the result of a computation on that data, you'll want to compose functions of type `a => Monad(b)`. Because the API calls are asynchronous, you'll need to wrap the return values in something like a promise or observable. In other words, the signatures for those functions are `a => Monad(b)`, and `b => Monad(c)`, respectively.

Composing functions of type `g: a => b, f: b => c` is easy because the types line up: `h: a => c` is just `a => f(g(a))`.

Composing functions of type `g: a => Monad(b), f: b => Monad(c)` is a little harder: `h: a => Monad(c)` is not just `a => f(g(a))` because `f` is expecting `b`, not `Monad(b)`.

Let's get a little more concrete and compose a pair of asynchronous functions that each return a promise:

```
{
  const label = 'Promise composition';

  const g = n => Promise.resolve(n + 1);
  const f = n => Promise.resolve(n * 2);

  const h = composePromises(f, g);

  h(20)
    .then(trace(label))
  ;
  // Promise composition: 42
}
```

How do we write `composePromises()` so that the result is logged correctly? *Hint: You've already seen it.*

Remember our `composeMap()` function? All you need to do is change the `.map()` call to `.then()`. `Promise.then()` is basically an asynchronous `.map()`.

```
{
  const composePromises = (...ms) => (
    ms.reduce((f, g) => x => g(x).then(f))
  );

  const label = 'Promise composition';

  const g = n => Promise.resolve(n + 1);
  const f = n => Promise.resolve(n * 2);

  const h = composePromises(f, g);

  h(20)
    .then(trace(label))
  ;
  // Promise composition: 42
}
```

The weird part is that when you hit the second function, `f` (remember, `f` *after* `g`), the input value is a promise. It's not type `b`, it's type `Promise(b)`, but `f` takes type `b`, unwrapped. So what's going on?

Inside `.then()`, there's an unwrapping process that goes from `Promise(b)` -> `b`. That operation is called **flatten** (aka join).

You may have noticed that composeMap() and composePromises() are almost identical functions. This is the perfect use-case for a higher-order function that can handle both. Let's just mix the flatMap method into a curried function, then use square bracket notation:

```
const composeM = method => (...ms) => (
  ms.reduce((f, g) => x => g(x)[method](f))
);
```

Now we can write the specialized implementations like this:

```
const composePromises = composeM('then');
const composeMap = composeM('map');
const composeFlatMap = composeM('flatMap');
```

The Monad Laws

Before you can start building your own monads, you need to know there are three laws that all monads should satisfy.

Left and right identity laws

The left and right identity laws are the symmetrical equalities:

- Left identity: *of then f = f*
- Right identity: *f then of = f*

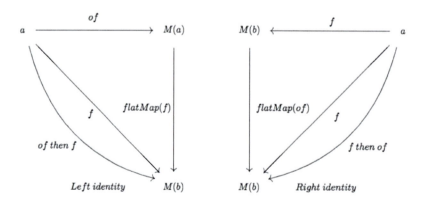

Left identity: *of then f = f* **Right identity:** *f = f then of*

Taken together:

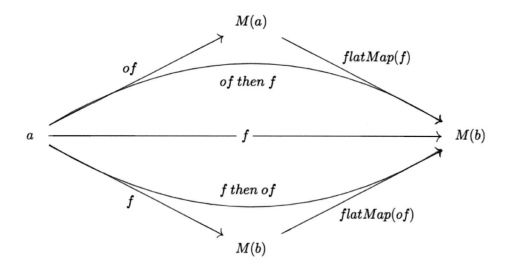

Monad left and right identity: *of then f = f = f then of*

If that first diagram looks familiar, that's not a coincidence. The monad laws are exactly the laws which define what a category is.

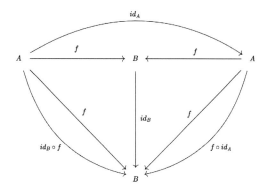

Category identity morphisms: $id_B \circ f = f = f \circ id_A$

All three of these diagrams are expressing the same general concept. The fact that monads obey the category laws is intentional. Monads form categories where objects are arrows and morphisms are functors between arrows (remember, functors map from category to category).

Associativity law

$$(f \text{ then } g) \text{ then } h = f \text{ then } (g \text{ then } h)$$

In JavaScript code, these laws can be expressed as:

1. Left identity: `of(x).flatMap(f)` ≡ `f(x)`
2. Right identity: `f(x).flatMap(of)` ≡ `f(x)`
3. Associativity: `of(x).flatMap(f).flatMap(g)` ≡ `of(x).flatMap(x => f(x).flatMap(g))`

Identity Laws

A monad is a functor. A functor is a morphism between two category objects, $A \to B$. The morphism is represented by an arrow between objects. In addition to the arrow we explicitly see between objects, each object in a category also has an arrow back to itself. In other words, for every object A in a category, there exists an arrow $A \to A$. That arrow is known as the identity arrow. It's frequently drawn as an arrow that loops back to the origin object.

Associativity

Associativity just means that it doesn't matter where we put the parenthesis when we compose. For example, if you're adding, $a + (b + c)$ is the same as $(a + b) + c$. The same holds true for function composition: $(f \circ g) \circ h = f \circ (g \circ h)$.

The same holds true for Kleisli composition. You just have to read it backwards. When you see the composition operator (`flatMap`), think `after`:

```
h(x).flatMap(x => g(x).flatMap(f))  ====  (h(x).flatMap(g)).flatMap(f)
```

Proving the Monad Laws

Let's prove that the identity monad satisfies the monad laws:

```
{ // Identity monad
  const Id = value => ({
    // Functor mapping
    // Preserve the wrapping for .map() by
    // passing the mapped value into the type
    // lift:
    map: f => Id.of(f(value)),

    // Monad chaining
    // Discard one level of wrapping
    // by omitting the .of() type lift:
    flatMap: f => f(value),
```

```
13
14      // Just a convenient way to inspect
15      // the values:
16      toString: () => `Id(${ value })`
17    });
18
19    // The type lift for this monad is just
20    // a reference to the factory.
21    Id.of = Id;
22
23    const g = n => Id(n + 1);
24    const f = n => Id(n * 2);
25
26    // Left identity
27    // unit(x).flatMap(f) ==== f(x)
28    trace('Id monad left identity')([
29      Id(x).flatMap(f),
30      f(x)
31    ]);
32    // Id monad left identity: Id(40), Id(40)
33
34
35    // Right identity
36    // m.flatMap(unit) ==== m
37    trace('Id monad right identity')([
38      Id(x).flatMap(Id.of),
39      Id(x)
40    ]);
41    // Id monad right identity: Id(20), Id(20)
42
43    // Associativity
44    // m.flatMap(f).flatMap(g) ====
45    // m.flatMap(x => f(x).flatMap(g)
46    trace('Id monad associativity')([
47      Id(x).flatMap(g).flatMap(f),
48      Id(x).flatMap(x => g(x).flatMap(f))
49    ]);
50    // Id monad associativity: Id(42), Id(42)
51  }
```

Conclusion

Monads are a way to compose type lifting functions: `g: a => M(b)`, `f: b => M(c)`. To accomplish this, monads must flatten `M(b)` to `b` before applying `f()`. In other words, functors are things you can map over. Monads are things you can flatMap over:

- Functions can compose: `a => b => c` becomes `a => c`
- Functors can compose functions with context: given `F(a)` and two functions, `a => b => c`, return `F(c)`.
- Monads can compose type lifting functions: `a => M(b)`, `b => M(c)` becomes `a => M(c)`

A monad is based on a simple symmetry — A way to wrap a value into a context, and a way to access the value in the context:

- **Lift/Unit**: A type lift from some type into the monad context: `a => M(a)`
- **Flatten/Join**: Unwrapping the type from the context: `M(c) => c` — this is usually the result of mapping `a => M(b)`, so `M(c) => c` is usually `M(M(b)) => M(b)`. The purpose of flatten is to discard the extra layer of wrapping.

And since monads are also functors, they can also map:

- **Map**: Map with context preserved: `M(a) -> M(b)`

Combine flatten with map, and you get flatMap — function composition for lifting functions, aka Kleisli composition:

- **FlatMap/Chain** Flatten + map: given `f: a => M(b)`, `g: b => M(c)` `f(a).map(g)` returns `M(M(b))`, so `f(a).map(g).flatten()` returns `M(b)`, which is the same as `f(a).flatMap(g)`.

Monads must satisfy three laws (axioms), collectively known as the monad laws:

- Left identity: `unit(x).flatMap(f)` ==== `f(x)`
- Right identity: `m.flatMap(unit)` ==== `m`
- Associativity: `m.flatMap(f).flatMap(g)` ==== `m.flatMap(x => f(x).flatMap(g))`

Examples of monads you might encounter in every day JavaScript code include promises and observables. Kleisli composition allows you to compose your data flow logic without worrying about the particulars of the data type's API, and without worrying about the possible side-effects, conditional branching, or other details of the unwrapping computations hidden in the `flatMap()` operation.

This makes monads a very powerful tool to simplify your code. You don't have to understand or worry about what's going on inside monads to reap the simplifying benefits that monads can provide, but now that you know more about what's under the hood, taking a peek under the hood isn't such a scary prospect.

No need to fear Lady Monadgreen's curse.

The Forgotten History of OOP

> "The Web as I envisaged it, we have not seen it yet. The future is still so much bigger than the past." ~ Tim Berners-Lee

Tim Berners-Lee once said "the future is still so much bigger than the past," but sometimes, the past lights the way. Since the early 1990s, one style of programming has dominated the thinking of software development teams: OOP. But do we really understand what OOP is, where it came from, or the goals and trade-offs that shaped its development? If you want to learn about something, it often helps to take a closer look at it in the historical context that shaped it.

Most of the programming paradigms we use today were first explored mathematically in the 1930s with lambda calculus and the Turing machine, which are alternative formulations of universal computation (formalized systems which can perform general computation). The Church Turing Thesis showed that lambda calculus and Turing machines are functionally equivalent — that anything that can be computed using a Turing machine can be computed using lambda calculus, and vice versa.

> Note: There is a common misconception that Turing machines can compute anything computable. There are classes of problems (e.g., the halting problem[36]) that can be computable for some cases, but are not generally computable for all cases using Turing machines. When I use the word "computable" in this text, I mean "computable by a Turing machine".

Lambda calculus represents a top-down, function application approach to computation, while the ticker tape/register machine formulation of the Turing machine represents a bottom-up, imperative (step-by-step) approach to computation.

Low level languages like machine code and assembly appeared in the 1940s, and by the end of the 1950s, the first popular high-level languages appeared. Lisp dialects are still in common use today, including Clojure, Scheme, AutoLISP, etc. FORTRAN and COBOL both appeared in the 1950s and are examples of imperative high-level languages still in use today, though C-family languages have replaced both COBOL and FORTRAN for most applications.

Both imperative programming and functional programming have their roots in the mathematics of computation theory, predating digital computers. "Object-Oriented Programming" (OOP) was coined by Alan Kay circa 1966 or 1967 while he was at grad school, but what we think of as OOP today is not the OOP that Alan Kay had in mind.

---

[36]https://en.wikipedia.org/wiki/Halting_problem

Ivan Sutherland's seminal Sketchpad application was an early inspiration for OOP. It was created between 1961 and 1962 and published in his Sketchpad Thesis in 1963[37]. The "objects" were data structures representing graphical images displayed on an oscilloscope screen, and featured inheritance via dynamic delegates, which Ivan Sutherland called "masters" in his thesis. Any object could become a master, and additional instances of the objects were called "occurrences". Many occurrences could then be composed together to form a drawing. Sketchpad's masters share a lot in common with JavaScript's prototypes.

One of the interesting features of Sketchpad was the constraint solver. For example, Sketchpad allowed the human artist to create two lines and then set a constraint that meant, "these lines should be parallel". Unlike most modern graphics applications, those relationships were solved for dynamically by minimizing the total error over the constraints. It was possible in Sketchpad to run simulations of things like how a bridge might behave under heavy loads or strong winds. Sketchpad was not just a drawing program — it was a dynamic simulation of object interactions.

> "The constraints and their integrated solvers presented 'programming a computer' in terms of 'whats' rather than 'hows'. The Sketchpad 'programmer' could *influence* values and histories, but only the internals of Sketchpad could effect the 'hows'. This made a big impression on me. [...] Life scales because the system dynamics of very large systems can be treated much more effectively by abandoning 'clockwork' and embracing dynamic reformulations and 'error attenuation.'" ~ Alan Kay in a 2018 email exchange.

Simula, specified in 1965 was another early influence on OOP. Alan Kay encountered Simula I the same week he learned about Sketchpad, in 1966. Like Sketchpad, Simula I could produce complex simulations from relatively little code. It also featured objects without class inheritance. Eventually, Simula 67 introduced class inheritance, subclasses, and virtual methods, which later appeared in languages like C++ and Java.

> Note: A **virtual method** is a method defined on a class which is designed to be overridden by subclasses. Virtual methods allow a program to call methods that may not exist at the moment the code is compiled by employing dynamic dispatch to determine what concrete method to invoke at runtime. JavaScript features dynamic types and uses the delegation chain to determine which methods to invoke, so does not need to expose the concept of virtual methods to programmers. Put another way, all methods in JavaScript use runtime method dispatch, so methods in JavaScript don't need to be declared "virtual" to support the feature.

The Big Idea

> "I made up the term 'object-oriented', and I can tell you I didn't have C++ in mind." ~ Alan Kay, OOPSLA '97

---

[37]https://dspace.mit.edu/handle/1721.1/14979

Alan Kay coined the term "object oriented programming" at grad school in 1966 or 1967. The big idea was to use encapsulated mini-computers in software which communicated via message passing rather than direct data sharing — to stop breaking down programs into separate "data structures" and "procedures".

> "The basic principal of recursive design is to make the parts have the same power as the whole." ~ Bob Barton, the main designer of the B5000, a mainframe optimized to run Algol-60.

> "For the first time I thought of the whole as the entire computer and wondered why anyone would want to divide it up into weaker things called data structures and procedures. Why not divide it up into little computers, as time sharing was starting to? But not in dozens. Why not thousands of them, each simulating a useful structure?" ~ Alan Kay, "The Early History of Smalltalk"[38]

Smalltalk was developed by Alan Kay, Dan Ingalls, Adele Goldberg, and others at Xerox PARC. Smalltalk was more object-oriented than Simula — everything in Smalltalk is an object, including classes, integers, and blocks (closures). The original Smalltalk-72 did not feature subclassing. That was introduced in Smalltalk-76 by Dan Ingalls[39].

While Smalltalk supported classes and eventually subclassing, Smalltalk was not about classes or subclassing things. It was a functional language inspired by more by Sketchpad and Lisp than Simula. Alan Kay considers the industry's focus on subclassing to be a distraction from the true benefits of object oriented programming.

> "I'm sorry that I long ago coined the term 'objects' for this topic because it gets many people to focus on the lesser idea. The big idea is messaging." ~ Alan Kay

In a 2003 email exchange[40], Alan Kay clarified what he meant when he called Smalltalk "object-oriented":

> "OOP to me means only messaging, local retention and protection and hiding of state-process, and extreme late-binding of all things." ~ Alan Kay

In other words, according to Alan Kay, the essential ingredients of OOP are:

- Message passing
- Encapsulation
- Dynamic binding

Notably, inheritance and subclass polymorphism were NOT considered essential ingredients of OOP by Alan Kay.

---

[38]http://worrydream.com/EarlyHistoryOfSmalltalk
[39]http://worrydream.com/EarlyHistoryOfSmalltalk
[40]http://www.purl.org/stefan_ram/pub/doc_kay_oop_en

The Essence of OOP

The combination of message passing and encapsulation serve some important purposes:

- **Encapsulating state** by isolating other objects from local state changes. The only way to affect another object's state is to ask (not command) that object to change it by sending a message. State changes are controlled at a local, cellular level rather than exposed to shared access.
- **Decoupling objects from each other** — the message sender is only loosely coupled to the message receiver, through the messaging API.
- **Runtime adaptability** via late binding. Runtime adaptability provides many great benefits that Alan Kay considered essential to OOP.

These ideas were inspired by biological cells and networked computers via Alan Kay's background in biology and influence from the design of Arpanet (an early version of the internet). Even that early on, Alan Kay imagined software running on a giant, distributed computer (like the internet), where individual computers acted like biological cells, operating independently on their own isolated state, and communicating via message passing. But he also thought that a local program could look like thousands of networked computers, too. The small parts could function the same way the large network functions, like a fractal.

> "I realized that the cell/whole-computer metaphor would get rid of data[...]" ~ Alan Kay

By "get rid of data", Alan Kay was surely aware of shared mutable state problems and tight coupling caused by shared dataâ€Š—â€Šcommon themes today.

But in the late 1960s, ARPA programmers were frustrated by the need to choose a data model[41] representation for their programs in advance of building software. Procedures that were too tightly coupled to particular data structures were not resilient to change or reusable. They wanted a more homogenous treatment of data.

> "[...] the whole point of OOP is not to have to worry about what is inside an object. Objects made on different machines and with different languages should be able to talk to each other[...]" ~ Alan Kay

Objects can abstract away and hide data structure implementations. The internal implementation of an object could change without breaking other parts of the software system. In fact, with extreme late binding, an entirely different computer system could take over the responsibilities of an object, and the software could keep working. Objects, meanwhile, could expose a standard interface that works with whatever data structure the object happened to use internally. The same interface could work with a linked list, a tree, a stream, and so on.

Alan Kay also saw objects as algebraic structures, which make certain mathematically provable guarantees about their behaviors:

---

[41]https://www.rand.org/content/dam/rand/pubs/research_memoranda/2007/RM5290.pdf

> "My math background made me realize that each object could have several algebras associated with it, and there could be families of these, and that these would be very very useful."

This has proven to be true, and forms the basis for objects such as promises and lenses, both inspired by category theory.

The algebraic nature of Alan Kay's vision for objects would allow objects to afford formal verifications, deterministic behavior, and improved testability, because algebras are essentially operations which obey a few rules in the form of equations.

In programmer lingo, algebras are like abstractions made up of functions (operations) accompanied by specific laws enforced by unit tests those functions must pass (axioms/equations).

You might say the programming world is rediscovering the benefits of functional programming and equational reasoning in context of modern general purpose languages after the software industry all but forgot about them for a few decades.

Like JavaScript and Smalltalk before it, most modern OO languages are becoming more and more multi-paradigm languages. There is no reason to choose between functional programming and OOP. When we look at the historical essence of each, they are not only compatible, but complementary ideas.

Because they share so many features in common, I like to say that JavaScript is Smalltalk's revenge on the world's misunderstanding of OOP. Both Smalltalk and JavaScript support:

- Objects
- First-class functions and closures
- Dynamic types
- Late binding (functions/methods changeable at runtime)
- OOP without class inheritance

What OOP Doesn't Mean

What is essential to OOP?

- Encapsulation
- Message passing
- Dynamic binding (the ability for the program to evolve/adapt at runtime)

What is non-essential?

- Classes
- Class inheritance

- Special treatment for objects/functions/data
- The new keyword
- Polymorphism
- Static types
- Recognizing a class as a "type"

If your background is Java or C#, you may be thinking static types and Polymorphism are essential ingredients, but Alan Kay preferred dealing with generic behaviors in algebraic form. For example, from Haskell:

```
fmap :: (a -> b) -> f a -> f b
```

This is the functor map signature, which acts generically over unspecified types a and b, applying a function from a to b in the context of a functor of a to produce a functor of b. Functor is math jargon that essentially means "supporting the map operation". If you're familiar with [].map() in JavaScript, you already know what that means.

Here are two examples in JavaScript:

```
// isEven = Number => Boolean
const isEven = n => n % 2 === 0;

const nums = [1, 2, 3, 4, 5, 6];

// map takes a function `a => b` and an array of `a`s (via `this`)
// and returns an array of `b`s.
// in this case, `a` is `Number` and `b` is `Boolean`
const results = nums.map(isEven);

console.log(results);
// [false, true, false, true, false, true]
```

The .map() method is generic in the sense that a and b can be any type, and .map() handles it just fine because arrays are data structures that implement the algebraic functor laws. The types don't matter to .map() because it doesn't try to manipulate them directly, instead applying a function that expects and returns the correct types for the application.

```
1  // matches = a => Boolean
2  // here, `a` can be any comparable type
3  const matches = control => input => input === control;
4
5  const strings = ['foo', 'bar', 'baz'];
6
7  const results = strings.map(matches('bar'));
8
9  console.log(results);
10 // [false, true, false]
```

This generic type relationship is difficult to express correctly and thoroughly in a language like TypeScript, but was pretty easy to express in Haskell's Hindley Milner types with support for higher kinded types (types of types).

Most type systems have been too restrictive to allow for free expression of dynamic and functional ideas, such as function composition, free object composition, runtime object extension, combinators, lenses, etc. In other words, static types frequently make it harder to write composable software.

If your type system is too restrictive (e.g., TypeScript, Java), you're forced to write more convoluted code to accomplish the same goals. That doesn't mean static types are a bad idea, or that all static type implementations are equally restrictive. I have encountered far fewer problems with Haskell's type system.

If you're a fan of static types and you don't mind the restrictions, more power to you, but if you find some of the advice in this text difficult because it's hard to type composed functions and composite algebraic structures, blame the type system, not the ideas. People love the comfort of their SUVs, but nobody complains that they don't let you fly. For that, you need a vehicle with more degrees of freedom.

If restrictions make your code simpler, great! But if restrictions force you to write more complicated code, perhaps the restrictions are wrong.

What is an object?

Objects have clearly taken on a lot of connotations over the years. What we call "objects" in JavaScript are simply composite data types, with none of the implications from either class-based programming or Alan Kay's message-passing.

In JavaScript, those objects can and frequently do support encapsulation, message passing, behavior sharing via methods, even subclass polymorphism (albeit using a delegation chain rather than type-based dispatch). You can assign any function to any property. You can build object behaviors dynamically, and change the meaning of an object at runtime. JavaScript also supports encapsulation using closures for implementation privacy. But all of that is opt-in behavior.

Our current idea of an object is simply a composite data structure, and does not require anything more to be considered an object. But programming using these kinds of objects does not make your code "object-oriented" any more than programming with functions makes your code "functional".

We've lost the plot.

Because "object" in modern programming languages means much less than it did to Alan Kay, I'm using "component" instead of "object" to describe what could be. Many objects are owned and manipulated directly by other code in JavaScript, but components should encapsulate and control their own state.

Characteristics of Message Passing

- Program with components (Alan Kay's "object")
- Encapsulate component state
- Use message passing for communication
- Add/change/replace components at runtime

Most component behaviors can be specified generically using algebraic data structures. Inheritance is not needed. Components can reuse behaviors from shared functions and modular imports without sharing their data.

In most modern software, there is some UI responsible for managing user interactions, some code managing application state (user data), and code managing system or network I/O.

Each of those systems may require long-lived processes, such as event listeners, state to keep track of things like the network connection, UI element status, and the application state itself.

Instead of all of these systems reaching out and directly manipulating each other's state, the system communicates with other components via message dispatch. When the user clicks on a save button, a `"SAVE"` message might get dispatched, which an application state component might interpret and relay to a state update handler (such as a pure reducer function). Perhaps after the state has been updated, the state component might dispatch a `"STATE_UPDATED"` message to a UI component, which in turn will interpret the state, reconcile what parts of the UI need to be updated, and relay the updated state to the subcomponents that handle those parts of the UI.

Meanwhile, the network connection component might be monitoring the user's connection to another machine on the network, listening for messages, and dispatching updated state representations to save data on a remote machine. It's internally keeping track of a network heartbeat pulse, whether the connection is currently online or offline, and so on.

These systems don't need to know about the details of the other parts of the system. Only about their individual, modular concerns. The system components are decomposable and recomposable. They implement standardized interfaces so that they are able to interoperate. As long as the interface is satisfied, you could substitute replacements which may do the same thing in different ways, or completely different things with the same messages. You may even do so at runtime, and everything would keep working properly.

Components of the same software system may not even need to be located on the same machine. The system could be decentralized. The network storage might shard the data across a decentralized storage system like IPFS[42], so that the user is not reliant on the health of any particular machine to ensure their data is safely stored.

OOP was partially inspired by Arpanet, and one of the goals of Arpanet was to build a decentralized network that could be resilient to network failures or attacks: An "Intergalactic Network" to hook all the ARPA project computers (and friends) together. According to director of DARPA during Arpanet development, Stephen J. Lukasik ("Why the Arpanet Was Built"[43]):

> "The goal was to exploit new computer technologies to meet the needs of military command and control against nuclear threats, achieve survivable control of US nuclear forces, and improve military tactical and management decision making."
>
> **Note**: The primary impetus of Arpanet was convenience rather than nuclear threat, and its obvious defense advantages emerged later. ARPA was using three separate computer terminals to communicate with three separate computer research projects. Bob Taylor wanted a single computer network to connect each project with the others.

It's possible using encapsulation and message passing to simulate the internet's robustness using components that are hot-swappable while the application is running. It could continue to work if the user is on a cell phone and they go offline because they entered a tunnel. It could continue to function if a hurricane knocks out the power to one of the data centers where servers are located.

It's possible, using these principles, to build more flexible, more resilient, better-composed software, using objects and functional programming in harmony.

> "If I have seen further it is by standing on the shoulders of Giants." ~ Isaac Newton

It often feels to me as if we've slipped off the giants' shoulders and got lost a bit too much in the implementation details of our OOP systems. I don't advocate going back to Smalltalk, but I wonder how much further we could see if we climb back on top of those shoulders.

---

[42]https://en.wikipedia.org/wiki/InterPlanetary_File_System
[43]https://ieeexplore.ieee.org/document/5432117

Object Composition

> "**Object Composition** Assembling or *composing* objects to get more complex behavior."
> ~ Gang of Four, "Design Patterns: Elements of Reusable Object-Oriented Software"[44]
>
> "Favor object composition over class inheritance." ~ Gang of Four, "Design Patterns".

One of the most common mistakes in software development is the tendency to overuse class inheritance. Class inheritance is a code reuse mechanism where instances form **is-a relations** with base classes. If you're tempted to model your domain using *is-a* relations (e.g., a duck *is-a* bird) you're bound for trouble, because class inheritance is the tightest form of coupling available in object-oriented design, which leads to many common problems, including (among others):

- The fragile base class problem
- The gorilla/banana problem
- The duplication by necessity problem

Class inheritance accomplishes reuse by abstracting a common interface away into a base class that subclasses can inherit from, add to, and override.

There are two important parts of **abstraction**:

- **Generalization** The process of extracting only the shared properties and behaviors that serve the general use case
- **Specialization** The process of providing the implementation details required to serve the special case

There are lots of ways to accomplish generalization and specialization in code. Some good alternatives to class inheritance include simple functions, higher order functions, modules, and object composition.

Unfortunately, object composition is very misunderstood, and many people struggle to think in terms of object composition, and even fail to recognize it when they see it and use it on a daily basis. It's time to explore the topic in a bit more depth.

---

[44]https://www.amazon.com/Design-Patterns-Elements-Reusable-Object-Oriented/dp/0201633612//ref=as_li_ss_tl?ie=UTF8&linkCode=ll1&tag=eejs-20&linkId=06ccc4a53e0a9e5ebd65ffeed9755744

What is Object Composition?

> "In computer science, a composite data type or compound data type is any data type which can be constructed in a program using the programming language's primitive data types and other composite types. [...] The act of constructing a composite type is known as composition." ~ Wikipedia

One of the reasons for the confusion surrounding object composition is that any assembly of primitive types to form a composite object is a form of object composition, but inheritance techniques are often discussed in contrast to object composition as if they are mutually exclusive things, e.g., "favor object composition over class inheritance." They're not. Class inheritance is a subset of object composition. The difference is more about intent than technique: Are we inheriting from a monolithic base class, or assembling smaller components to form a new composite?

When discussing object composition vs class inheritance, we're not talking about specific techniques: We're talking about the *semantic relationships* and *degree of coupling* between the component objects. We're talking about *meaning* as opposed to *technique*. People often fail to make the distinction and get mired in the technique details. They can't see the forest for the trees.

There are many different ways to compose objects. Different forms of composition will produce different composite structures and different relationships between the objects. When objects depend on the objects they're related to, those objects are coupled, meaning that changing one object could break the other.

The Gang of Four advice to "favor object composition over class inheritance" invites us to think of our objects as a composition of smaller, loosely coupled objects rather than wholesale inheritance from a monolithic base class. The GoF describes tightly coupled objects as "monolithic systems, where you can't change or remove a class without understanding and changing many other classes. The system becomes a dense mass that's hard to learn, port, and maintain."

Another source of confusion is that in most OO languages, a big distinction is made between data and functions. In most functional languages, functions and data get passed around interchangably.

The reason this distinction is important is because objects as Alan Kay described them for Smalltalk (which influenced all major OO languages that followed, including C++, Java, Objective C and C#) exist to solve the problem of shared mutable state. They accomplish that goal by controlling access to data via encapsulation (where functions outside the object can't directly observe or manipulate the object's private state), and message passing (the mechanism we use to communicate with objects - method calls are the simplest form).

When we asseble objects via composition, we don't care about any of that. We're just assembling data structures, treating methods and properties as data.

Three Different Forms of Object Composition

In "Design Patterns", the Gang of Four states, "you'll see object composition applied again and again in design patterns", and goes on to describe various types of compositional relationships, including *aggregation* and *delegation*.

The authors of "Design Patterns" were primarily working with C++ and Smalltalk (later Java). In those languages, it was relatively difficult to build objects up by extending them at runtime, so the GoF have little to say about dynamic object extension, AKA *concatenation*. However, it is one of the most common object composition techniques in JavaScript.

There are many kinds of objects and many data structures can be created using object composition, but there are three fundamental techniques that form the basis of all other forms of object composition:

- **Aggregation** When an object is formed from an enumerable collection of subobjects. In other words, an object which *contains* other objects. Each subobject retains its own reference identity, such that it could be destructured from the aggregation without information loss.
- **Concatenation** When an object is formed by adding new properties to an existing object. Properties can be concatenated one at a time or copied from existing objects, e.g., jQuery plugins are created by concatenating new methods to the jQuery delegate prototype, `jQuery.fn`.
- **Delegation** When an object forwards or *delegates to* another object. e.g., Ivan Sutherland's Sketchpad[45] (1962) included instances with references to "masters" which were delegated to for shared properties. Photoshop includes "smart objects" that serve as local proxies which delegate to an external resource. JavaScript's prototypes are also delegates: Array instances forward built-in array method calls to `Array.prototype`, objects to `Object.prototype`, etc...

It's important to note that these different forms of composition are not mutually exclusive. It's possible to implement delegation using aggregation, and class inheritance is implemented using delegation in JavaScript. Many software systems use more than one type of composition, e.g., jQuery's plugins use concatenation to extend the jQuery delegate prototype, `jQuery.fn`. When client code calls a plugin method, the request is delegated to the method that was concatenated to the delegate prototype.

Notes on Code Examples

The code examples below will share the following setup code:

---

[45]https://www.youtube.com/watch?v=BKM3CmRqK2o

```
1  const objs = [
2    { a: 'a', b: 'ab' },
3    { b: 'b' },
4    { c: 'c', b: 'cb' }
5  ];
```

All code examples of object composition will be written in the form of reducer functions. This is certainly not the only way to do it, but it is convenient, and very widely used to assemble and manage data structures of all kinds in a variety of programming languages.

Reduce is a higher order function which takes a function and applies it over a collection of items. In the case of object composition, the items in question are source objects, and we're reducing the collection of source objects to a single target object for output.

Reducers take the form:

```
1  (accumulator, currentValue) => accumulator
```

With each iteration, the new current value gets folded into the accumulator, where "fold" is not a single, well defined operation, but the operation suplied by the reducer function body.

The classic summing example:

```
1  const sum = (a, c) => a + c;
2
3  const total = [1,2,3].reduce(sum, 0);
4  // => 6
```

And a basic object composition example, using concatenation via object spread syntax:

```
1  const assign = (a, c) => ({...a, ...c});
2
3  const composed = [{a: 'a'}, {b: 'b'}].reduce(assign, {});
4  // => { a: 'a', b: 'b' }
```

Aggregation

Aggregation is when an object is formed from an enumerable collection of subobjects. An aggregate is an object which *contains* other objects. Each subobject in an aggregation retains its own reference identity, and could be losslessly destructured from the aggregate. Aggregates can be represented in a wide variety of structures.

Examples

- Arrays
- Maps
- Sets
- Graphs
- Trees
    - DOM nodes (a DOM node may *contain* child nodes)
    - UI components (a component may *contain* child components)

When to use

Whenever there are collections of objects which need to share common operations, such as iterables, stacks, queues, trees, graphs, state machines, or the composite pattern (when you want a single item to share the same interface as many items).

Considerations

Aggregations are great for applying universal abstractions, such as applying a function to each member of an aggregate (e.g., `array.map(fn)`), transforming vectors as if they're single values, and so on. If there are potentially hundreds of thousands or millions of subobjects, however, stream processing or delegation may be more efficient.

In Code

Array aggregation:

```
const collection = (a, e) => a.concat([e]);

const a = objs.reduce(collection, []);

console.log(
  'collection aggregation',
  a,
  a[1].b,
  a[2].c,
  `enumerable keys: ${ Object.keys(a) }`
);
```

This will produce:

```
1  collection aggregation
2  [{"a":"a","b":"ab"},{"b":"b"},{"c":"c","b":"cb"}]
3  b c
4  enumerable keys: 0,1,2
```

Linked list aggregation using pairs:

```
1  const pair = (a, b) => [b, a];
2
3  const l = objs.reduceRight(pair, []);
4
5  console.log(
6    'linked list aggregation',
7    l,
8    `enumerable keys: ${ Object.keys(l) }`
9  );
10
11 /*
12 linked list aggregation
13 [
14   {"a":"a","b":"ab"}, [
15     {"b":"b"}, [
16       {"c":"c","b":"cb"},
17       []
18     ]
19   ]
20 ]
21 enumerable keys: 0,1
22 */
```

Linked lists form the basis of lots of other data structures and aggregations, such as arrays, strings, and various kinds of trees. The DOM tree is based on linked lists, with DOM nodes pointing to children, children nodes pointing back to parents, and delegated references to sibling nodes. There are many other possible kinds of aggregation. We won't cover them all in-depth here.

Concatenation

Concatenation is when an object is formed by adding new properties to an existing object.

Examples

- Plugins are added to `jQuery.fn` via concatenation

- State reducers (e.g., Redux)
- Functional mixins

When to Use

Any time it would be useful to progressively assemble data structures at runtime, e.g., merging JSON objects, hydrating application state from multiple sources, creating updates to immutable state (by merging previous state with new data), etc…

Considerations

- Be careful mutating existing objects. Shared mutable state is a recipe for many bugs.
- It's possible to mimic class hierarchies and **is-a relations** with concatenation. The same problems apply. Think in terms of composing small, independent objects rather than inheriting props from a "base" instance and applying differential inheritance.
- Beware of implicit inter-component dependencies.
- Property name collisions are resolved by concatenation order: last-in wins. This is useful for defaults/overrides behavior, but can be problematic if the order shouldn't matter.

In Code

```
const concatenate = (a, o) => ({...a, ...o});

const c = objs.reduce(concatenate, {});

console.log(
  'concatenation',
  c,
  `enumerable keys: ${ Object.keys(c) }`
);

// concatenation { a: 'a', b: 'cb', c: 'c' } enumerable keys: a,b,c
```

Delegation

Delegation is when an object forwards or *delegates to* another object.

Examples

- JavaScript's built-in types use delegation to forward built-in method calls up the prototype chain. e.g., `[].map()` delegates to `Array.prototype.map()`, `obj.hasOwnProperty()` delegates to `Object.prototype.hasOwnProperty()` and so on.
- jQuery plugins rely on delegation to share built-in and plugin methods among all jQuery object instances.
- Sketchpad's "masters" were dynamic delegates. Modifications to the delegate would be reflected instantly in all of the object instances.
- Photoshop uses delegates called "smart objects" to refer to images and resources defined in separate files. Changes to the object that smart objects refer to are reflected in all instances of the smart object.

When to Use

1. **Conserve memory**: Any time there may be potentially many instances of an object and it would be useful to share identical properties or methods among each instance which would otherwise require allocating more memory.
2. **Dynamically update many instances**: Any time many instances of an object need to share identical state which may need to be updated dynamically and changes instantaneously reflected in every instance, e.g., Sketchpad's "masters" or Photoshop's "smart objects".

Considerations

- Delegation is commonly used to imitate class inheritance in JavaScript (wired up by the `extends` keyword), but is very rarely actually needed.
- Delegation can be used to exactly mimic the behavior and limitations of class inheritance. In fact, class inheritance in JavaScript is built on top of static delegates via the prototype delegation chain. Avoid **is-a** thinking.
- Delegate props are non-enumerable using common mechanisms such as `Object.keys(instanceObj)`.
- Delegation saves memory at the cost of property lookup performance, and some JS engine optimizations get turned off for dynamic delegates (delegates that change after they've been created). However, even in the slowest case, property lookup performance is measured in millions of ops per second – chances are good that this is not your bottleneck unless you're building a utility library for object operations or graphics programming, e.g., RxJS or three.js.
- Need to differentiate between instance state, and delegate state.
- Shared state on dynamic delegates is not instance safe. Changes are shared between all instances. Shared state on dynamic delegates is commonly (but not always) a bug.
- ES6 classes don't create dynamic delegates in ES6. They may seem to work in Babel, but will fail hard in real ES6 environments.

In Code

```
 1  const delegate = (a, b) => Object.assign(Object.create(a), b);
 2
 3  const d = objs.reduceRight(delegate, {});
 4
 5  console.log(
 6    'delegation',
 7    d,
 8    `enumerable keys: ${ Object.keys(d) }`
 9  );
10
11  // delegation { a: 'a', b: 'ab' } enumerable keys: a,b
12
13  console.log(d.b, d.c); // ab c
```

Conclusion

We have learned:

- All objects made from other objects and language primitives are *composite objects.*
- The act of creating a composite object is known as *object composition.*
- There are different kinds of object composition.
- The relationships and dependencies we form when we compose objects differ depending on how objects are composed.
- *Is-a relations* (the kind formed by class inheritance) are the tightest form of coupling in OO design, and should generally be avoided when its practical.
- The Gang of Four admonishes us to compose objects by assembling smaller features to form a larger whole, rather than inheriting from a monolithic base class or base object. "Favor object composition over class inheritance."
- Aggregation composes objects into enumerable collections where each member of the collection retains its own identity, e.g., arrays, DOM tree, etc...
- Delegation composes objects by linking together an object delegation chain where an object forwards or delegates property lookups to another object. e.g., [].map() delegates to Array.prototype.map()
- Concatenation composes objects by extending an existing object with new properties, e.g., Object.assign(destination, a, b), {...a, ...b}.
- The definitions of different kinds of object composition are **not mutually exclusive**. Delegation is a subset of aggregation, concatenation can be used to form delegates and aggregates, and so on...

These are not the only three kinds of object composition. It's also possible to form loose, dynamic relationships between objects through acquaintance/association relationships where objects are passed as parameters to other objects (dependency injection), and so on.

All software development is composition. There are easy, flexible ways to compose objects, and brittle, arthritic ways. Some forms of object composition form loosely coupled relations between objects, and others form very tight coupling.

Look for ways to compose where a small change to program requirements would require only a small change to the code implementation. Express your intention clearly and concisely, and remember: If you think you need class inheritance, chances are very good that there's a better way to do it.

Factory Functions

A factory function is any function which is not a class or constructor that returns a (presumably new) object. In JavaScript, any function can return an object. When it does so without the new keyword, it's a factory function.

Factory functions have always been attractive in JavaScript because they offer the ability to easily produce object instances without diving into the complexities of classes and the new keyword.

JavaScript provides a very handy object literal syntax. It looks something like this:

```javascript
const user = {
  userName: 'echo',
  avatar: 'echo.png'
};
```

Like JSON (which is based on JavaScript's object literal notation), the left side of the : is the property name, and the right side is the value. You can access props with dot notation:

```javascript
console.log(user.userName); // "echo"
```

You can access computed property names using square bracket notation:

```javascript
const key = 'avatar';
console.log( user[key] ); // "echo.png"
```

If you have variables in-scope with the same name as your intended property names, you can omit the colon and the value in the object literal creation:

```javascript
const userName = 'echo';
const avatar = 'echo.png';

const user = {
  userName,
  avatar
};

console.log(user);
// { "avatar": "echo.png", "userName": "echo" }
```

Object literals support concise method syntax. We can add a `.setUserName()` method:

```
1  const userName = 'echo';
2  const avatar = 'echo.png';
3
4  const user = {
5    userName,
6    avatar,
7    setUserName (userName) {
8      this.userName = userName;
9      return this;
10   }
11 };
12
13 console.log(user.setUserName('Foo').userName); // "Foo"
```

In concise methods, `this` refers to the object which the method is called on. To call a method on an object, simply access the method using object dot notation and invoke it by using parentheses, e.g., `game.play()` would apply `.play()` to the game object. In order to apply a method using dot notation, that method must be a property of the object in question. You can also apply a method to any other arbitrary object using the function prototype methods, `.call()`, `.apply()`, or `.bind()`.

In this case, `user.setUserName('Foo')` applies `.setUserName()` to user, so `this === user`. In the `.setUserName()` method, we change the `.userName` property on the `user` object via its `this` binding, and return the same object instance for method chaining.

Literals for One, Factories for Many

If you need to create many objects, you'll want to combine the power of object literals and factory functions.

With a factory function, you can create as many user objects as you want. If you're building a chat app, for instance, you can have a user object representing the current user, and also a lot of other user objects representing all the other users who are currently signed in and chatting, so you can display their names and avatars, too.

Let's turn our user object into a `createUser()` factory:

```
 1  const createUser = ({ userName, avatar }) => ({
 2    userName,
 3    avatar,
 4    setUserName (userName) {
 5      this.userName = userName;
 6      return this;
 7    }
 8  });
 9
10  console.log(createUser({ userName: 'echo', avatar: 'echo.png' }));
11  /*
12  {
13    "avatar": "echo.png",
14    "userName": "echo",
15    "setUserName": [Function setUserName]
16  }
17  */
```

Returning Objects

Arrow functions (=>) have an implicit return feature: if the function body consists of a single expression, you can omit the return keyword: `() => 'foo'` is a function that takes no parameters, and returns the string, `"foo"`.

Be careful when you return object literals. By default, JavaScript assumes you want to create a function body when you use braces, e.g., `{ broken: true }`. If you want to use an implicit return for an object literal, you'll need to disambiguate by wrapping the object literal in parentheses:

```
1  const noop = () => { foo: 'bar' };
2  console.log(noop()); // undefined
3
4  const createFoo = () => ({ foo: 'bar' });
5  console.log(createFoo()); // { foo: "bar" }
```

In the first example, `foo:` is interpreted as a label, and `bar` is interpreted as an expression that doesn't get assigned or returned. The function returns `undefined`.

In the `createFoo()` example, the parentheses force the braces to be interpreted as an expression to be evaluated, rather than a function body block.

Destructuring

Pay special attention to the function signature:

```
1  const createUser = ({ userName, avatar }) => ({
```

In this line, the braces (`{`, `}`) represent object destructuring. This function takes one argument (an object), but destructures two formal parameters from that single argument, `userName`, and `avatar`. Those parameters can then be used as variables in the function body scope. You can also destructure arrays:

```
1  const swap = ([first, second]) => [second, first];
2  console.log( swap([1, 2]) ); // [2, 1]
```

And you can use the rest and spread syntax (`...varName`) to gather the rest of the values from the array (or a list of arguments), and then spread those array elements back into individual elements:

```
1  const rotate = ([first, ...rest]) => [...rest, first];
2  console.log( rotate([1, 2, 3]) ); // [2, 3, 1]
```

Computed Property Keys

Earlier we used square bracket computed property access notation to dynamically determine which object property to access:

```
1  const key = 'avatar';
2  console.log( user[key] ); // "echo.png"
```

We can also compute the value of keys to assign to:

```
1  const arrToObj = ([key, value]) => ({ [key]: value });
2  console.log( arrToObj([ 'foo', 'bar' ]) ); // { "foo": "bar" }
```

In this example, `arrToObj()` takes an array consisting of a key/value pair (aka a tuple) and converts it into an object. Since we don't know the name of the key, we need to compute the property name in order to set the key/value pair on the object. For that, we borrow the idea of square bracket notation from computed property accessors, and reuse it in the context of building an object literal:

```
1  { [key]: value }
```

After the interpolation is done, we end up with the final object:

```
1  { "foo": "bar" }
```

Default Parameters

Functions in JavaScript support default parameter values, which have several benefits:

- Users are able to omit parameters with suitable defaults.
- The function is more self-documenting because default values supply examples of expected input.
- IDEs and static analysis tools can use default values to infer the type expected for the parameter. For example, a default value of 1 implies that the parameter can take a member of the Number type.

Using default parameters, we can document the expected interface for our createUser factory, and automatically fill in 'Anonymous' details if the user's info is not supplied:

```
1   const createUser = ({
2     userName = 'Anonymous',
3     avatar = 'anon.png'
4   } = {}) => ({
5     userName,
6     avatar
7   });
8
9   console.log(
10    // { userName: "echo", avatar: 'anon.png' }
11    createUser({ userName: 'echo' }),
12    // { userName: "Anonymous", avatar: 'anon.png' }
13    createUser()
14  );
```

The last part of the function signature probably looks a little funny:

```
1   } = {}) => ({
```

The last = {} bit just before the parameter signature closes means that if nothing gets passed in for this parameter, we're going to use an empty object as the default. When you try to destructure values from the empty object, the default values for properties will get used automatically, because that's what default values do: replace undefined with some predefined value.

Without the = {} default value, calling createUser() with no arguments would throw an error because you can't try to access properties from undefined.

Type Inference

JavaScript does not have any native type annotations as of this writing, but several competing formats have sprung up over the years to fill the gaps, including JSDoc (in decline due to the emergence of better options), Facebook's Flow[46], and Microsoft's TypeScript[47]. I use rtype[48] for documentation—a notation I find much more readable than TypeScript for functional programming.

At the time of this writing, there is no clear winner for type annotations. None of the alternatives have been blessed by the JavaScript specification, and there seem to be clear shortcomings in all of them.

Type inference is the process of inferring types based on the context in which they are used. In JavaScript, it is a very good alternative to type annotations.

If you provide enough clues for inference in your standard JavaScript function signatures, you'll get most of the benefits of type annotations with none of the costs or risks.

Even if you decide to use a tool like TypeScript or Flow, you should do as much as you can with type inference, and save the type annotations for situations where type inference falls short. For example, there's no native way in JavaScript to specify a shared interface. That's both easy and useful with TypeScript or rtype.

Tern.js is a popular type inference tool for JavaScript that has plugins for many code editors and IDEs.

Microsoft's Visual Studio Code doesn't need Tern because it brings the type inference capabilities of TypeScript to regular JavaScript code.

When you specify default parameters for functions in JavaScript, tools capable of type inference such as Tern.js, TypeScript, and Flow can provide IDE hints to help you use the API you're working with correctly.

Without defaults, IDEs (and frequently, humans) don't have enough hints to figure out the expected parameter type.

---

[46] https://flow.org/
[47] https://www.typescriptlang.org/
[48] https://github.com/ericelliott/rtype

```
1    const createUser = ({
2      userName,
3      avatar
4    } = {}) => ({
5      userName,
6      avatar
7    });
8
9    const foo = createUser({ user })
10
```

IDE screenshot: unknown type for `userName`.

With defaults, IDEs (and frequently, humans) can infer the types from the examples.

```
1  const createUser = ({
2    userName = 'Anonymous',
3    avatar = 'anon.png'
4  } = {}) => ({
5    userName,
6    avatar
7  });
8
9  const foo = createUser({ user})
10                              p   string  userName
```

IDE screenshot: `userName` is expecting a string.

It doesn't always make sense to restrict a parameter to a fixed type (that would make generic functions and higher order functions difficult), but when it does make sense, default parameters are often the best way to do it, even if you're using TypeScript or Flow.

Factory Functions for Mixin Composition

Factories are great at cranking out objects using a nice calling API. Usually, they're all you need, but once in a while, you'll find yourself building similar features into different types of objects, and you may want to abstract those features into functional mixins so you can reuse them more easily.

That's where functional mixins shine. Let's build a `withConstructor` mixin to add the `.constructor` property to all object instances.

```
1  // withConstructor.js
2  const withConstructor = constructor => o => ({
3    // create the delegate [[Prototype]]
4    __proto__: {
5      // add the constructor prop to the new [[Prototype]]
6      constructor
7    },
8    // mix all o's props into the new object
9    ...o
10 });
```

Now you can import it and use it with other mixins:

```
1  import withConstructor from `./with-constructor';
2
3  const pipe = (...fns) => x => fns.reduce((y, f) => f(y), x);
4  // or `import pipe from 'lodash/fp/flow';`
5
6  // Set up some functional mixins
7  const withFlying = o => {
8    let isFlying = false;
9    return {
10     ...o,
11     fly () {
12       isFlying = true;
13       return this;
14     },
15     land () {
16       isFlying = false;
17       return this;
18     },
19     isFlying: () => isFlying
20   }
21 };
22
23 const withBattery = ({ capacity }) => o => {
24   let percentCharged = 100;
25   return {
26     ...o,
27     draw (percent) {
28       const remaining = percentCharged - percent;
29       percentCharged = remaining > 0 ? remaining : 0;
30       return this;
```

```
31      },
32      getCharge: () => percentCharged,
33      getCapacity: () => capacity
34    };
35  };
36
37  const createDrone = ({ capacity = '3000mAh' }) => pipe(
38    withFlying,
39    withBattery({ capacity }),
40    withConstructor(createDrone)
41  )({});
42
43  const myDrone = createDrone({ capacity: '5500mAh' });
44
45  console.log(`
46    can fly:  ${ myDrone.fly().isFlying() === true }
47    can land: ${ myDrone.land().isFlying() === false }
48    battery capacity: ${ myDrone.getCapacity() }
49    battery status: ${ myDrone.draw(50).getCharge() }%
50    battery drained: ${ myDrone.draw(75).getCharge() }% remaining
51  `);
52
53  console.log(`
54    constructor linked: ${ myDrone.constructor === createDrone }
55  `);
```

As you can see, the reusable `withConstructor()` mixin is simply dropped into the pipeline with other mixins. `withBattery()` could be used with other kinds of objects, like robots, electric skateboards, or portable device chargers. `withFlying()` could be used to model flying cars, rockets, or air balloons.

Composition is more of a way of thinking than a particular technique in code. You can accomplish it in many ways. Function composition is just the easiest way to build it up from scratch, and factory functions are a simple way to wrap a friendly API around the implementation details.

Conclusion

ES6 provides a convenient syntax for dealing with object creation and factory functions. Most of the time, that's all you'll need, but because this is JavaScript, there's another approach that makes it feel more like Java: the `class` keyword.

In JavaScript, classes are more verbose & restrictive than factories, and a bit of a minefield when it comes to refactoring, but they've also been embraced by major front-end frameworks like React and Angular, and there are a couple of rare use-cases that make the complexity worthwhile.

"Sometimes, the elegant implementation is just a function. Not a method. Not a class. Not a framework. Just a function." ~ John Carmack

Start with the simplest implementation, and move to more complex implementations only as required.

Functional Mixins

Functional mixins are composable factory functions which connect together in a pipeline; each function adding some properties or behaviors like workers on an assembly line. Functional mixins don't depend on or require a base factory or constructor: Simply pass any arbitrary object into a mixin, and an enhanced version of that object will be returned.

Functional mixin features:

- Data privacy/encapsulation
- Inheriting private state
- Inheriting from multiple sources
- No diamond problem (property collision ambiguity) – last in wins
- No base-class requirement

Motivation

All modern software development is really composition: We break a large, complex problem down into smaller, simpler problems, and then compose solutions to form an application.

The atomic units of composition are one of two things:

- Functions
- Data structures

Application structure is defined by the composition of those atomic units. Often, composite objects are produced using class inheritance, where a class inherits the bulk of its functionality from a parent class, and extends or overrides pieces. The problem with that approach is that it leads to **is-a** thinking, e.g., "an admin is an employee", causing lots of design problems:

- **The tight coupling problem**: Because child classes are dependent on the implementation of the parent class, class inheritance is the tightest coupling available in object oriented design.
- **The fragile base class problem**: Due to tight coupling, changes to the base class can potentially break a large number of descendant classes—potentially in code managed by third parties. The author could break code they're not aware of.
- **The inflexible hierarchy problem**: With single ancestor taxonomies, given enough time and evolution, all class taxonomies are eventually wrong for new use-cases.

- **The duplication by necessity problem**: Due to inflexible hierarchies, new use cases are often implemented by duplication, rather than extension, leading to similar classes which are unexpectedly divergent. Once duplication sets in, it's not obvious which class new classes should descend from, or why.
- **The gorilla/banana problem**: "...the problem with object-oriented languages is they've got all this implicit environment that they carry around with them. You wanted a banana but what you got was a gorilla holding the banana and the entire jungle." ~ Joe Armstrong, "Coders at Work"[49]

If an admin is an employee, how do you handle a situation where you hire an outside consultant to perform administrative duties temporarily? If you knew every requirement in advance, perhaps class inheritance could work, but I've never seen that happen. Given enough usage, applications and requirements inevitably grow and evolve over time as new problems and more efficient processes are discovered.

Mixins offer a more flexible approach.

What are mixins?

> "Favor object composition over class inheritance" the Gang of Four, "Design Patterns: Elements of Reusable Object Oriented Software"[50]

Mixins are a form of object composition, where component features get mixed into a composite object so that properties of each mixin become properties of the composite object.

The term "mixins" in OOP comes from mixin ice cream shops. Instead of having a whole lot of ice-cream flavors in different pre-mixed buckets, you have vanilla ice cream, and a bunch of separate ingredients that could be mixed in to create custom flavors for each customer.

Object mixins are similar: You start with an empty object and mix in features to extend it. Because JavaScript supports dynamic object extension and objects without classes, using object mixins is trivially easy in JavaScript – so much so that it is the most common form of inheritance in JavaScript by a huge margin. Let's look at an example:

---

[49]http://www.amazon.com/gp/product/1430219483?ie=UTF8&camp=213733&creative=393185&creativeASIN=1430219483&linkCode=shr&tag=eejs-20&linkId=3MNWRRZU3C4Q4BDN

[50]https://www.amazon.com/Design-Patterns-Elements-Reusable-Object-Oriented/dp/0201633612/ref=as_li_ss_tl?ie=UTF8&qid=1494993475&sr=8-1&keywords=design+patterns&linkCode=ll1&tag=eejs-20&linkId=6c553f16325f3939e5abadd4ee04e8b4

```
const chocolate = {
  hasChocolate: () => true
};

const caramelSwirl = {
  hasCaramelSwirl: () => true
};

const pecans = {
  hasPecans: () => true
};

const iceCream = Object.assign({}, chocolate, caramelSwirl, pecans);

/*
// or, if your environment supports object spread...
const iceCream = {...chocolate, ...caramelSwirl, ...pecans};
*/

console.log(`
  hasChocolate: ${ iceCream.hasChocolate() }
  hasCaramelSwirl: ${ iceCream.hasCaramelSwirl() }
  hasPecans: ${ iceCream.hasPecans() }
`);
```

Which logs:

```
hasChocolate: true
hasCaramelSwirl: true
hasPecans: true
```

What is functional inheritance?

Functional inheritance is the process of inheriting features by applying an augmenting function to an object instance. The function supplies a closure scope which you can use to keep some data private. The augmenting function uses dynamic object extension to extend the object instance with new properties and methods.

Let's look at an example from Douglas Crockford, who coined the term:

```javascript
// Base object factory
function base(spec) {
    var that = {}; // Create an empty object
    that.name = spec.name; // Add it a "name" property
    return that; // Return the object
}

// Construct a child object, inheriting from "base"
function child(spec) {
    var that = base(spec); // Create the object through the "base" constructor
    that.sayHello = function() { // Augment that object
        return 'Hello, I\'m ' + that.name;
    };
    return that; // Return it
}

// Usage
var result = child({ name: 'a functional object' });
console.log(result.sayHello()); // 'Hello, I'm a functional object'
```

Because `child()` is tightly coupled to `base()`, when you add `grandchild()`, `greatGrandchild()`, etc..., you'll opt into most of the common problems from class inheritance.

What is a functional mixin?

Functional mixins are composable functions which mix new properties or behaviors into existing objects. Functional mixins don't depend on or require a base factory or constructor: Simply pass any arbitrary object into a mixin, and it will be extended.

Let's look at an example:

```javascript
const flying = o => {
  let isFlying = false;

  return Object.assign({}, o, {
    fly () {
      isFlying = true;
      return this;
    },

    isFlying: () => isFlying,
```

```
12      land () {
13        isFlying = false;
14        return this;
15      }
16    });
17  };
18
19  const bird = flying({});
20  console.log( bird.isFlying() ); // false
21  console.log( bird.fly().isFlying() ); // true
```

Notice that when we call `flying()`, we need to pass an object in to be extended. Functional mixins are designed for function composition. Let's create something to compose with:

```
1  const quacking = quack => o => Object.assign({}, o, {
2    quack: () => quack
3  });
4
5  const quacker = quacking('Quack!')({});
6  console.log( quacker.quack() ); // 'Quack!'
```

Composing Functional Mixins

Functional mixins can be composed with simple function composition:

```
1  const createDuck = quack => quacking(quack)(flying({}));
2
3  const duck = createDuck('Quack!');
4
5  console.log(duck.fly().quack());
```

That looks a little awkward to read, though. It can also be a bit tricky to debug or re-arrange the order of composition.

Of course, this is standard function composition, and we already know some better ways to do that using `compose()` or `pipe()`. If we use `pipe()` to reverse the function order, the composition will read like `Object.assign({}, ...)` or `{...object, ...spread}` – preserving the same order of precedence. In case of property collisions, the last object in wins.

```
1  const pipe = (...fns) => x => fns.reduce((y, f) => f(y), x);
2  // OR...
3  // import pipe from `lodash/fp/flow`;
4
5  const createDuck = quack => pipe(
6    flying,
7    quacking(quack)
8  )({});
9
10 const duck = createDuck('Quack!');
11
12 console.log(duck.fly().quack());
```

When to Use Functional Mixins

You should always use the simplest possible abstraction to solve the problem you're working on. Start with a pure function. If you need an object with persistent state, try a factory function. If you need to build more complex objects, try functional mixins.

Here are some good use-cases for functional mixins:

- Application state management, e.g., something similar to a Redux store.
- Certain cross-cutting concerns and services, e.g., a centralized logger.
- Composable functional data types, e.g., the JavaScript `Array` type implements `Semigroup`, `Functor`, `Foldable`... Some algebraic structures can be derived in terms of other algebraic structures, meaning that certain derivations can be composed into a new data type without customization.

React users: `class` is fine for lifecycle hooks because callers aren't expected to use `new`, and documented best-practice is to avoid inheriting from any components other than the React-provided base components.

I use and recommend HOCs (Higher Order Components) with function composition to compose UI components.

Caveats

Most problems can be elegantly solved using pure functions. The same is not true of functional mixins. Like class inheritance, functional mixins can cause problems of their own. In fact, it's possible to faithfully reproduce all of the features and problems of class inheritance using functional mixins.

You can avoid that, though, using the following advice:

- Favor pure functions > factories > functional mixins > classes
- Avoid the creation of *is-a* relationships between objects, mixins, or data types
- Avoid implicit dependencies between mixins – wherever possible, functional mixins should be self-contained, and have no knowledge of other mixins
- "Functional mixins" doesn't mean "functional programming"
- There may be side-effects when you access a property using `Object.assign()` or object spread syntax (`{...object}`). You'll also skip any non-enumerable properties. ES2017 added `Object.getOwnPropertyDescriptors()` to get around this problem.

I rely mostly on function composition to compose behavior and application structure, but frequently use functional mixins in the form of Higher Order Components (HOCs) (which mix into component properties) and Express middleware (which mix into the request and response objects).

Note: React recently announced React hooks: a function-based approach to effects and component state. Hooks provide a much clearer abstraction than the class lifecycle methods did. Class lifecycle methods will continue to work, but if you're tempted to use classes in React, you should consider hooks, instead.

Classes

Class inheritance is very rarely (perhaps *never*) the best approach in JavaScript, but that choice is sometimes made by a library or framework that you don't control. In that case, using `class` is sometimes practical, provided the library:

1. Does not require you to extend your own classes (i.e., does not require you to build multi-level class hierarchies), and
2. Does not require you to directly use the `new` keyword – in other words, the framework handles instantiation for you

Both Angular 2+ and React meet those requirements, so you can safely use classes with them, as long as you don't extend your own classes. React allows you to avoid using classes if you wish, but your components may fail to take advantage of optimizations built into React's base classes, and your components won't look like the components in documentation examples. In any case, you should always prefer the function form for React components when it makes sense.

Class Performance

In some browsers, classes may provide JavaScript engine optimizations that are not available otherwise. In almost all cases, those optimizations will not have a significant impact on your app's performance. In fact, it's possible to go many years without ever needing to worry about `class` performance differences. Object creation and property access is always very fast (millions of ops/sec), regardless of how you build your objects.

That said, authors of general purpose utility libraries similar to RxJS, Lodash, etc... should investigate possible performance benefits of using `class` to create object instances. Unless you have measured a significant bottleneck that you can provably and substantially reduce using `class`, you should optimize for clean, flexible code instead of worrying about performance.

Implicit Dependencies

You may be tempted to create functional mixins designed to work together. Imagine you want to build a configuration manager for your app that logs warnings when you try to access configuration properties that don't exist.

It's possible to build it like this:

```
const pipe = (...fns) => x => fns.reduce((y, f) => f(y), x);

// in its own module...
const withLogging = logger => o => Object.assign({}, o, {
  log (text) {
    logger(text)
  }
});


// in a different module with no explicit mention of
// withLogging -- we just assume it's there...
const withConfig = config => (o = {
  log: (text = '') => console.log(text)
}) => Object.assign({}, o, {
  get (key) {
    return config[key] == undefined ?

      // vvv implicit dependency here... oops! vvv
      this.log(`Missing config key: ${ key }`) :
      // ^^^ implicit dependency here... oops! ^^^

      config[key]
    ;
  }
});

// in yet another module that imports withLogging and
// withConfig...
const createConfig = ({ initialConfig, logger }) =>
```

```javascript
31    pipe(
32      withLogging(logger),
33      withConfig(initialConfig)
34    )({})
35  ;
36
37  // elsewhere...
38  const initialConfig = {
39    host: 'localhost'
40  };
41
42  const logger = console.log.bind(console);
43
44  const config = createConfig({initialConfig, logger});
45
46  console.log(config.get('host')); // 'localhost'
47  config.get('notThere'); // 'Missing config key: notThere'
```

However, it's also possible to build it like this:

```javascript
1   const pipe = (...fns) => x => fns.reduce((y, f) => f(y), x);
2
3   // import withLogging() explicitly in withConfig module
4   import withLogging from './with-logging';
5
6   const addConfig = config => o => Object.assign({}, o, {
7     get (key) {
8       return config[key] == undefined ?
9         this.log(`Missing config key: ${ key }`) :
10        config[key]
11      ;
12    }
13  });
14
15  const withConfig = ({ initialConfig, logger }) => o =>
16    pipe(
17
18      // vvv compose explicit dependency in here vvv
19      withLogging(logger),
20      // ^^^ compose explicit dependency in here ^^^
21
22      addConfig(initialConfig)
23    )(o)
```

```
24  ;
25
26  // The factory only needs to know about withConfig now...
27  const createConfig = ({ initialConfig, logger }) =>
28    withConfig({ initialConfig, logger })({})
29  ;
30
31
32  // elsewhere, in a different module...
33  const initialConfig = {
34    host: 'localhost'
35  };
36
37  const logger = console.log.bind(console);
38
39  const config = createConfig({initialConfig, logger});
40
41  console.log(config.get('host')); // 'localhost'
42  config.get('notThere'); // 'Missing config key: notThere'
```

The correct choice depends on a lot of factors. It is valid to require a lifted data type for a functional mixin to act on, but if that's the case, the API contract should be made explicitly clear in the function signature and API documentation.

That's the reason that the implicit version has a default value for o in the signature. Since JavaScript lacks type annotation capabilities, we can fake it by providing default values:

```
1  const withConfig = config => (o = {
2    log: (text = '') => console.log(text)
3  }) => Object.assign({}, o, {
```

This tells the reader, "the o argument should be an object with a log() method that takes a string".

If you're using TypeScript or Flow, it's probably better to declare an explicit interface for your o requirements.

Functional Mixins & Functional Programming

"Functional" in the context of functional mixins does not always have the same purity connotations as "functional programming". Functional mixins are commonly used in OOP style, complete with side-effects. Many functional mixins will alter the object argument you pass to them. Caveat emptor.

By the same token, some developers prefer a functional programming style, and will not maintain an identity reference to the object you pass in. You should code your mixins and the code that uses them assuming a random mix of both styles.

That means that if you need to return the object instance, always return `this` instead of a reference to the instance object in the closure – in functional code, chances are those are not references to the same objects. Additionally, always assume that the object instance will be copied by assignment using `Object.assign()` or `{...object, ...spread}` syntax. That means that if you set non-enumerable properties, they will probably not work on the final object:

```
const a = Object.defineProperty({}, 'a', {
  enumerable: false,
  value: 'a'
});

const b = {
  b: 'b'
};

console.log({...a, ...b}); // { b: 'b' }
```

By the same token, if you're using functional mixins that you didn't create in your functional code, don't assume the code is pure. Assume that the base object may be mutated, and assume that there may be side-effects & no referential transparency guarantees, i.e., it is frequently unsafe to memoize factories composed of functional mixins.

Conclusion

Functional mixins are composable factory functions which add properties and behaviors to objects like stations in an assembly line. They are a great way to compose behaviors from multiple source features (*has-a*, *uses-a*, *can-do*), as opposed to inheriting all the features of a given class (*is-a*).

Be aware, "functional mixins" doesn't imply "functional programming" – it simply means, "mixins using functions". Functional mixins can be written using a functional programming style, avoiding side-effects and preserving referential transparency, but that is not guaranteed. There may be side-effects and nondeterminism.

- Unlike simple object mixins, functional mixins support true data privacy (encapsulation), including the ability to inherit private data.
- Unlike single-ancestor class inheritance, functional mixins also support the ability to inherit from many ancestors, similar to class decorators, traits, or multiple inheritance.
- Unlike multiple inheritance in C++, the diamond problem is rarely problematic in JavaScript, because there is a simple rule when collisions arise: The last mixin added wins.
- Unlike class decorators, traits, or multiple inheritance, no base class is required.

Favor the simplest implementation over more complex constructions:

Pure functions > factory functions > functional mixins > classes

Why Composition is Harder with Classes

Previously, we examined factory functions and looked at how easy it is to use them for composition using functional mixins. Now we're going to look at classes in more detail, and examine how the mechanics of class get in the way of composition.

We'll also take a look at the good use-cases for classes and how to use them safely.

ES6 includes a convenient class syntax, so you may be wondering why we should care about factories at all. The most obvious difference is that constructors and class require the new keyword. But what does new actually do?

- Creates a new object and binds this to it in the constructor function.
- Implicitly returns this, unless you explicitly return another object.
- Sets the instance [[Prototype]], instance.__proto__ to Constructor.prototype, so that Object.getPrototypeOf(instance) === Constructor.prototype and instance.__proto__ === Constructor.prototype.
- Sets the instance.constructor === Constructor.

All of that implies that, unlike factory functions, classes are not a good solution for composing functional mixins. You can still achieve composition using class, but it's a much more complex process, and as you'll see, the additional costs are usually not worth the extra effort.

The Delegate Prototype

You may eventually need to refactor from a class to a factory function, and if you require callers to use the new keyword, that refactor could break client code you're not even aware of in a couple of ways: First, unlike classes and constructors, factory functions don't automatically wire up a delegate prototype link.

The [[Prototype]] link is used for prototype delegation, which is a convenient way to conserve memory if you have millions of objects, or to squeeze a micro-performance boost out of your program if you need to access tens of thousands of properties on an object within a 16 ms render loop cycle.

If you don't need to micro-optimize memory or performance, the [[Prototype]] link can do more harm than good. The prototype chain powers the instanceof operator in JavaScript, and unfortunately instanceof lies for two reasons:

In ES5, the `Constructor.prototype` link was dynamic and reconfigurable, which could be a handy feature if you need to create an abstract factory—but if you reassign the prototype, `instanceof` will give you false negatives if the `Constructor.prototype` does not currently reference the same object in memory that the instance `[[Prototype]]` references:

```javascript
class User {
  constructor ({userName, avatar}) {
    this.userName = userName;
    this.avatar = avatar;
  }
}

const currentUser = new User({
  userName: 'Foo',
  avatar: 'foo.png'
});

User.prototype = {};

console.log(
  currentUser instanceof User, // <-- false -- Oops!
  // But it clearly has the correct shape:
  // { avatar: "foo.png", userName: "Foo" }
  currentUser
);
```

Chrome solves the problem by making the `Constructor.prototype` property `configurable: false` in the property descriptor. However, Babel (a popular JavaScript compiler) does not currently mirror that behavior, so Babel compiled code will behave like ES5 constructors. V8 silently fails if you attempt to reconfigure the `Constructor.prototype` property. Either way, you won't get the results you expected. Worse: the behavior is inconsistent, and code that works now in Babel is likely to break in the future.

I don't recommend reassigning `Constructor.prototype`.

A more common problem is that JavaScript has multiple execution contexts called *realms*—memory sandboxes where the same code will access different physical memory locations. For example, if you have a constructor in a parent frame and the same constructor in an iframe, the parent frame's `Constructor.prototype` will not reference the same memory location as the `Constructor.prototype` in the iframe. Object values in JavaScript are memory references under the hood, and different frames point to different locations in memory, so `===` checks will fail.

Another problem with `instanceof` is that it is a nominal type check rather than a structural type check, which means that if you start with a class and later switch a factory, all the calling code using `instanceof` won't understand new implementations even if they satisfy the same interface contract. For example, say you're tasked with building a music player interface. Later on the product team tells you to add support for videos. Later still, they ask you to add support for 360 videos. They all supply the same controls: play, stop, rewind, fast forward.

But if you're using `instanceof` checks, members of your video interface class won't satisfy the `foo instanceof AudioInterface` checks already in the codebase.

They'll fail when they should succeed. Sharable interfaces in other languages solve this problem by allowing a class to declare that it implements a specific interface. That's not currently possible in JavaScript.

The best way to deal with `instanceof` in JavaScript is to break the delegate prototype link if it's not required, and let `instanceof` fail for every call. That way you won't get a false sense of reliability. Don't listen to `instanceof`, and it will never lie to you.

The `.constructor` Property

The `.constructor` property is a rarely used feature in JavaScript, but it could be very useful, and it's a good idea to include it on your object instances. It's mostly harmless if you don't try to use it for type checking (which is unsafe for the same reasons instanceof is unsafe).

In theory, `.constructor` could be useful to make generic functions which are capable of returning a new instance of whatever object you pass in.

In practice, there are many different ways to create new instances of things in JavaScript—having a reference to the constructor is not the same thing as knowing how to instantiate a new object with it—even for seemingly trivial purposes, such as creating an empty instance of a given object:

```javascript
// Return an empty instance of any object type?
const empty = ({ constructor } = {}) => constructor ?
  new constructor() :
  undefined
;

const foo = [10];

console.log(
  empty(foo) // []
);
```

It seems to work with Arrays. Let's try it with Promises:

```
// Return an empty instance of any type?
const empty = ({ constructor } = {}) => constructor ?
  new constructor() :
  undefined
;

const foo = Promise.resolve(10);

console.log(
  empty(foo) // [TypeError: Promise resolver undefined is
             //   not a function]
);
```

Note the new keyword in the code. That's most of the problem. It's not safe to assume that you can use the new keyword with any factory function. Sometimes, that will cause errors.

What we would need to make this work is to have a standard way to pass a value into a new instance using a standard factory function that doesn't require new. There is a specification for that: a static method on any factory or constructor called .of(). The .of() method is a factory that returns a new instance of the data type containing whatever you pass into .of().

We could use .of() to create a better version of the generic empty() function:

```
// Return an empty instance of any type?
const empty = ({ constructor } = {}) => constructor.of ?
  constructor.of() :
  undefined
;

const foo = [23];

console.log(
  empty(foo) // []
);
```

Unfortunately, the static .of() method is just beginning to gain support in JavaScript. The Promise object does have a static method that acts like .of(), but it's called .resolve() instead, so our generic empty() won't work with promises:

```javascript
// Return an empty instance of any type?
const empty = ({ constructor } = {}) => constructor.of ?
  constructor.of() :
  undefined
;

const foo = Promise.resolve(10);

console.log(
  empty(foo) // undefined
);
```

Likewise, there's no .of() for strings, numbers, objects, maps, weak maps, or sets in JavaScript as of this writing.

If support for the .of() method catches on in other standard JavaScript data types, the .constructor property could eventually become a much more useful feature of the language. We could use it to build a rich library of utility functions capable of acting on a variety of functors, monads, and other algebraic datatypes.

It's easy to add support for .constructor and .of() to a factory:

```javascript
const createUser = ({
  userName = 'Anonymous',
  avatar = 'anon.png'
} = {}) => ({
  userName,
  avatar,
  constructor: createUser
});
createUser.of = createUser;

// testing .of and .constructor:
const empty = ({ constructor } = {}) => constructor.of ?
  constructor.of() :
  undefined
;

const foo = createUser({ userName: 'Empty', avatar: 'me.png' });

console.log(
  empty(foo), // { avatar: "anon.png", userName: "Anonymous" }
  foo.constructor === createUser.of, // true
```

```
22      createUser.of === createUser    // true
23  );
```

You can even make `.constructor` non-enumerable by adding to the delegate prototype:

```
1   const createUser = ({
2     userName = 'Anonymous',
3     avatar = 'anon.png'
4   } = {}) => ({
5     __proto__: {
6       constructor: createUser
7     },
8     userName,
9     avatar
10  });
```

Class to Factory is a Breaking Change

Factories allow increased flexibility because they:

- Decouple instantiation details from calling code.
- Allow you to return arbitrary objects—for instance, to use an object pool to tame the garbage collector.
- Don't pretend to provide any type guarantees, so callers are less tempted to use instanceof and other unreliable type checking measures, which might break code across execution contexts, or if you switch to an abstract factory.
- Can dynamically swap implementations for abstract factories. e.g., a media player that swaps out the `.play()` method for different media types.
- Adding capability with composition is easier with factories.

While it's possible to accomplish most of these goals using classes, it's easier to do so with factories. There are fewer potential bug pitfalls, less complexity to juggle, and a lot less code.

For these reasons, it's often desirable to refactor from a class to a factory, but it can be a complex, error prone process. Refactoring from classes to factories is a common need in every OO language. You can read more about it in "Refactoring: Improving the Design of Existing Code"[51] by Martin Fowler, Kent Beck, John Brant, William Opdyke, and Don Roberts.

Due to the fact that new changes the behavior of a function being called, changing from a class or constructor to a factory function is a potentially breaking change. In other words, forcing callers to

---

[51]https://www.amazon.com/Refactoring-Improving-Design-Existing-Code/dp/0201485672/ref=as_li_ss_tl?ie=UTF8&linkCode=ll1&tag=eejs-20&linkId=dec737e066f3a92e46c7e493692cbb0a&language=en_US

use new could unwittingly lock callers into the constructor implementation, so new leaks potentially breaking implementation details into the calling API.

Internally, you'll also need to be mindful that this may be dynamically bound from factory call sites, which is not the case when callers use new. That can complicate matters if you want to store alternate abstract factory prototypes as static properties on the factory.

There is another problem, too. All class callers must use new. Leaving it off in ES6 will always throw:

```
class Foo {};

// TypeError: Class constructor Foo cannot be invoked without 'new'
const Bar = Foo();
```

In ES6+, arrow functions are commonly used to create factories, but because arrow functions don't have their own this binding in JavaScript, invoking an arrow function with new throws an error:

```
const foo = () => ({});

// TypeError: foo is not a constructor
const bar = new foo();
```

So, if you try to refactor from a class to an arrow function factory, it will fail in native ES6 environments, which is OK. Failing hard is a good thing.

But, if you compile arrow functions to standard functions, it will *fail to fail*. That's bad, because it should be an error. It will "work" while you're building the app, but potentially fail in production where it could impact the user experience, or even prevent the app from working at all.

A change in the compiler default settings could break your app, even if you didn't change any of your own code. That gotcha bears repeating:

> **Warning**: Refactoring from a class to an arrow function factory might seem to work with a compiler, but if the code compiles the factory to a native arrow function, your app will break because you can't use new with arrow functions.

As we have already seen, the following implicit behaviors can make the switch a breaking change:

- Absence of the [[Prototype]] link from factory instances will break caller instanceof checks.
- Absence of the .constructor property from factory instances could break code that relies on it.
- Callers using new could begin to throw errors or experience unexpected behavior after switching to a factory.

Code that Requires `new` Violates the Open/Closed Principle

Our APIs should be *open to extension,* but *closed to breaking changes.* Since a common extension to a class is to turn it into a more flexible factory, but that refactor is a breaking change, code that requires the `new` keyword is *closed to extension* and *open to breaking changes.* That's the opposite of what we want.

The impact of this is larger than it seems at first. If your class API is public, or if you work on a very large app with a very large team, the refactor is likely to break code you're not even aware of. It's a better idea to deprecate the class entirely and replace it with a factory function to move forward.

That process changes a small technical problem that can be solved silently by code into an unbounded people problem that requires awareness, education, and buy-in—a much more expensive change!

I've seen the `new` issue cause very expensive headaches many times, and it's trivially easy to avoid:

> Export a factory instead of a class.

The `class` Keyword and `extends`

The class keyword is supposed to be a nicer syntax for object creation patterns in JavaScript, but it falls short in several ways:

Friendly Syntax

The primary purpose of class was to provide a friendly syntax to mimic class from other languages in JavaScript. The question we should ask ourselves though is, does JavaScript really need to mimic class from other languages?

JavaScript's factory functions provide a friendlier syntax out of the box, with much less complexity. Often, an object literal is good enough. If you need to create many instances, factories are a good next step.

In Java and C++, factories are more complicated than classes, but they're often worth building anyway because they provide enhanced flexibility. In JavaScript, factories are less complicated and more flexible than classes.

Compare the class:

```javascript
1  class User {
2    constructor ({userName, avatar}) {
3      this.userName = userName;
4      this.avatar = avatar;
5    }
6  }
7
8  const currentUser = new User({
9    userName: 'Foo',
10   avatar: 'foo.png'
11 });
```

Vs the equivalent factory:

```javascript
1  const createUser = ({ userName, avatar }) => ({
2    userName,
3    avatar
4  });
5
6  const currentUser = createUser({
7    userName: 'Foo',
8    avatar: 'foo.png'
9  });
```

With JavaScript and arrow function familiarity, factories are clearly less syntax and easier to read. Maybe you prefer to see the new keyword, but there are good reasons to avoid new. Familiarity bias may be holding you back.

Performance and Memory

`class` offers two kinds of performance optimizations: shared memory for properties stored on the delegate prototype, and property lookup optimizations.

Good use cases for delegate prototypes are rare. `class` syntax is a little nicer than the equivalent syntax for ES5 constructor functions, but the primary purpose is to hook up the delegate prototype chain, and good use cases for delegate prototypes are rare. It really boils down to performance.

The delegate prototype memory optimization is available to both factories and classes. A factory can set the prototype by setting the `__proto__` property in an object literal or by using `Object.create(proto)`. Even so, most modern devices have RAM measured in gigabytes. Before using a delegate prototype, you should profile and make sure it's really needed.

`class` property lookup optimizations are tiny microoptimizations. Any type of closure scope or property access is measured in hundreds of thousands or millions of ops/second, so performance differences are rarely measurable in the context of an application, let alone impactful.

There are exceptions, of course. RxJS used class instances because they were faster than closure scopes when they profiled, but RxJS is a general purpose utility library that might be used in the context of hundreds of thousands operations that need to be squeezed into a 16ms render loop.

ThreeJS uses classes, but ThreeJS is a 3d rendering library which might be used for game engines manipulating thousands of objects every 16ms.

It makes sense for libraries like ThreeJS and RxJS to go to extremes optimizing wherever they can.

In the context of applications, we should *avoid premature optimization,* and focus our efforts only where they'll make a large impact. For most applications, that means our network calls and payloads, animations, asset caching strategies, etc.

Don't micro-optimize for performance unless you've noticed a performance problem, profiled your application code, and pinpointed a real bottleneck.

Instead, you should optimize code for maintenance and flexibility.

Type Checking

Classes in JavaScript are dynamic, and instanceof checks don't work across execution contexts, so type checking based on `class` is a non-starter. It's unreliable. It's likely to cause bugs and make your application unnecessarily rigid.

Class Inheritance with `extends`

Class inheritance causes several well-known problems that bear repeating:

- **Tight coupling**: Class inheritance is the tightest form of coupling available in object-oriented design.
- **Inflexible hierarchies**: Given enough time and users, all class hierarchies are eventually wrong for new use cases, but tight coupling makes refactors difficult.
- **Gorilla/Banana problem**: No selective inheritance. "You wanted a banana but what you got was a gorilla holding the banana and the entire jungle." ~ Joe Armstrong in "Coders at Work"[52]
- **Duplication by necessity**: Due to inflexible hierarchies and the gorilla/banana problem, code reuse is often accomplished by copy/paste, violating DRY (Don't Repeat Yourself) and defeating the entire purpose of inheritance in the first place.

The only purpose of `extends` is to create single-ancestor class taxonomies. Some clever hacker will read this and say, "Ah hah! Not so! You can do class composition!" To which I would answer, "ah, but now you're using object composition instead of class inheritance, and there are easier, safer ways to do that in JavaScript without extends."

---

[52]https://www.amazon.com/Coders-Work-Reflections-Craft-Programming/dp/1430219483/ref=as_li_ss_tl?ie=UTF8&linkCode=ll1&tag=eejs-20&linkId=bba2355edc3c24d87ecf2901fb91a473&language=en_US

Classes are OK if You're Careful

With all the warnings out of the way, some clear guidelines emerge that can help you use classes safely:

- **Avoid `instanceof`**—it lies because JavaScript is dynamic and has multiple execution contexts, and instanceof fails in both situations. It can also cause problems if you switch to an abstract factory down the road.
- **Avoid `extends`**—don't extend a single hierarchy more than once. "Favor object composition over class inheritance." ~ "Design Patterns: Elements of Reusable Object-Oriented Software"[53]
- **Avoid exporting your class**. Use `class` internally for performance gains, but export a factory that creates instances in order to discourage users from extending your class and avoid forcing callers to use `new`.
- **Avoid `new`**. Try to avoid using it directly whenever it makes sense, and don't force your callers to use it. (Export a factory, instead).

It's OK to use class if:

- **You're building UI components for a framework like React or Angular**. Both frameworks wrap your component classes into factories and manage instantiation for you, so you don't have to use `new` in your own code.
- **You never inherit from your own classes or components**. Instead, try object composition, function composition, higher order functions, higher order components, or modules—all of them are better code reuse patterns than class inheritance.
- **You need to optimize performance**. Just remember to export a factory so callers don't have to use `new` and don't get lured into the extends trap.

In most other situations, factories will serve you better.

Factories are simpler than classes or constructors in JavaScript. Always start with the simplest solution and progress to more complex solutions only as-needed.

---

[53]https://www.amazon.com/Design-Patterns-Elements-Reusable-Object-Oriented/dp/0201633612/ref=as_li_ss_tl?ie=UTF8&linkCode=ll1&tag=eejs-20&linkId=f5bc273a996c30f845cc99d929523abf&language=en_US

Composable Custom Data Types

In JavaScript, the easiest way to compose is function composition, and a function is just an object you can add methods to. In other words, you can do this:

```
const t = value => {
  const fn = () => value;

  fn.toString = () => `t(${ value })`;

  return fn;
};


const someValue = t(2);

console.log(
  someValue.toString() // "t(2)"
);
```

This is a factory that returns instances of a numerical data type, t. But notice that those instances aren't simple objects. Instead, they're functions, and like any other function, you can compose them. Let's assume the primary use case for it is to sum its members. Maybe it would make sense to sum them when they compose.

The following code won't work yet, because we haven't finished building our type, so for now just imagine you have a value of the type, t(0). That value is itself a function, and when you pass another value of the same type into the returned function, it will add the two values together and return the summed value of the same type. In other words:

```
console.log(
  t(3)(t(5)).toString() // t(8)
);
```

Before we implement the needed changes, let's establish some rules (axioms):

- Identity: $t(x)(t(0)) \equiv t(x)$
- Associativity: $t(a)(t(b))(t(c)) \equiv t(a)(t(b)(t(c)))$ $(a + b) + c = a + (b + c)$

Note: ≡ means "is equivalent to".

You can express this in JavaScript using the convenient `.toString()` method we already created:

- `t(x)(t(0)).toString() === t(x).toString()`
- `t(a)(t(b))(t(c)).toString() === t(a)(t(b)(t(c))).toString()`

And we can translate those into a simple kind of unit test:

```
const assert = ({given, should, actual, expected}) => {
  if (actual.toString() !== expected.toString()) {
    throw new Error(`NOT OK: Given ${ given }, should ${ should }
      Expected: ${ expected }
      Actual:   ${ actual }
    `);
  }

  console.log(`OK: Given ${ given }, should ${ should }`);
};


{
  const given = 'a value `t(x)` composed with `t(0)`';
  const should = 'be equivalent to `t(x)`';
  const x = 20;

  const actual = t(x)(t(0));
  const expected = t(x);

  assert({
    given,
    should,
    actual,
    expected
  });
}

{
  const given = 'a value `t(x)` composed with `t(1)`';
  const should = 'be equivalent to `t(x + 1)`';
  const [a, b, c] = [1, 2, 3];

```

```
34    const actual = t(x)(t(1));
35    const expected = t(x + 1);
36
37    assert({
38      given,
39      should,
40      actual,
41      expected
42    });
43  }
```

These tests will fail at first:

```
1  NOT OK: a value t(x) composed with t(0) ==== t(x)
2          Expected: t(20)
3          Actual:   20
```

But we can make them pass with 3 simple steps:

1. Change the `fn` function into an `add` function that returns `t(value + n)` where `n` is the passed argument.
2. Add a `valueOf()` method to the `t` type so that the new `add()` function can take instances of `t()` as arguments. The `+` operator will use the result of `n.valueOf()` as the second operand.
3. Assign the methods to the `add()` function with `Object.assign()`.

When you put it all together, it looks like this:

```
1  const t = value => {
2    const add = n => t(value + n);
3
4    return Object.assign(add, {
5      toString: () => `t(${ value })`,
6      valueOf: () => value
7    });
8  };
```

And then the tests pass:

```
1  "OK: a value t(x) composed with t(0) ==== t(x)"
2  "OK: a value t(x) composed with t(1) ==== t(x + 1)"
```

Now you can compose values of `t()` with function composition:

```
1   // Compose functions from top to bottom:
2   const pipe = (...fns) => x => fns.reduce((y, f) => f(y), x);
3
4   // Sugar to kick off the pipeline with an initial value:
5   const add = (...fns) => pipe(...fns)(t(0));
6
7   const sum = add(
8     t(2),
9     t(4),
10    t(-1)
11  );
12
13  console.log(sum.toString()) // t(5)
```

You can do this with any data type

It doesn't matter what shape your data takes, as long as there is some composition operation that makes sense. For lists or strings, it could be concatenation. For Digial Signal Processing (DSP), it could be signal summing. Of course lots of different operations might make sense for the same data. The question is, which operation best represents the concept of composition? In other words, which operation would benefit most expressed like this?:

```
1   const result = compose(
2     value1,
3     value2,
4     value3
5   );
```

Composable Currency

Moneysafe[54] is an open source library that implements this style of composable functional datatypes. JavaScript's `Number` type can't accurately represent certain fractions of dollars.

```
1   .1 + .2 === .3 // false
```

Moneysafe solves the problem by lifting dollar amounts to cents:

---

[54]https://github.com/ericelliott/moneysafe

```
npm install --save moneysafe
```

Then:

```
import { $ } from 'moneysafe';

$(.1) + $(.2) === $(.3).cents; // true
```

The ledger syntax takes advantage of the fact that Moneysafe lifts values into composable functions. It exposes a simple function composition utility called the ledger:

```
import { $ } from 'moneysafe';
import { $$, subtractPercent, addPercent } from 'moneysafe/ledger';

$$(
  $(40),
  $(60),
  // subtract discount
  subtractPercent(20),
  // add tax
  addPercent(10)
).$; // 88
```

The returned value is a value of the lifted money type. It exposes the convenient `.$` getter which converts the internal floating-point cents value into dollars, rounded to the nearest cent.

The result is an intuitive interface for performing ledger-style money calculations.

Lenses

A lens is a composable pair of pure getter and setter functions which focus on a particular field inside an object, and obey a set of axioms known as the lens laws. Think of the object as the *whole* and the field as the *part*. The getter takes a whole and returns the part of the object that the lens is focused on.

```
1  // view = whole => part
```

The setter takes a whole, and a value to set the part to, and returns a new whole with the part updated. Unlike a function which simply sets a value into an object's member field, Lens setters are pure functions:

```
1  // set = whole => part => whole
```

> **Note:** In this text, we're going to use some naive lenses in the code examples just to give you a beneath-the-hood peek at the general concept. For production code, you should look at a well tested library like Ramda, instead. The API differs between different lens libraries, and it's possible to express lenses in more composable, elegant ways than they are presented here.

Imagine you have a tuple array representing a point's x, y, and z coordinates:

```
1  [x, y, z]
```

To get or set each field individually, you might create three lenses. One for each axis. You could manually create getters which focus on each field:

```
1  const getX = ([x]) => x;
2  const getY = ([x, y]) => y;
3  const getZ = ([x, y, z]) => z;
4
5  console.log(
6    getZ([10, 10, 100]) // 100
7  );
```

Likewise, the corresponding setters might look like this:

```javascript
const setY = ([x, _, z]) => y => ([x, y, z]);

console.log(
  setY([10, 10, 10])(999) // [10, 999, 10]
);
```

Why Lenses?

State shape dependencies are a common source of coupling in software. Many components may depend on the shape of some shared state, so if you need to later change the shape of that state, you have to change logic in multiple places.

Lenses allow you to abstract state shape behind getters and setters. Instead of littering your codebase with code that dives deep into the shape of a particular object, import a lens. If you later need to change the state shape, you can do so in the lens, and none of the code that depends on the lens will need to change.

This follows the principle that a small change in requirements should require only a small change in the system.

Background

In 1985, "Structure and Interpretation of Computer Programs"[55] described getter and setter pairs (called put and get in the text) as a way to isolate an object's shape from the code that uses the object. The text shows how to create generic selectors that access parts of a complex number independent of how the number is represented. That isolation is useful because it breaks state shape dependencies. These getter/setter pairs were a bit like referenced queries which have existed in relational databases for decades.

Lenses took the concept further by making getter/setter pairs more generic and composable. They were popularized after Edward Kmett released the Lens library for Haskell. He was influenced by Jeremy Gibbons and Bruno C. d. S. Oliveira, who demonstrated that traversals express the iterator pattern, Luke Palmer's "accessors", Twan van Laarhoven, and Russell O'Connor.

> **Note:** An easy mistake to make is to equate the modern notion of a functional lens with Anamorphisms, based on Erik Meijer, Maarten Fokkinga, and Ross Paterson's "Functional Programming with Bananas, Lenses, Envelopes and Barbed Wire"[56] in 1991. "The term 'lens' in the functional reference sense refers to the fact that it looks at part of a whole. The term 'lens' in a recursion scheme sense refers to the fact that [(and)] syntactically look

---

[55]https://www.amazon.com/Structure-Interpretation-Computer-Programs-Engineering/dp/0262510871/ref=as_li_ss_tl?ie=UTF8&linkCode=ll1&tag=eejs-20&linkId=9fac31d60f8b9b60f63f71ab716694bc
[56]http://citeseerx.ist.psu.edu/viewdoc/summary?doi=10.1.1.41.125

kind of like concave lenses. **tl;dr** They have nothing to do with one another." ~ Edward Kmett on Stack Overflow[57]

Lens Laws

The lens laws are algebraic axioms which ensure that the lens is well behaved.

1. `view(lens, set(lens, value, store)) ≡ value` — If you set a value into the store, and immediately view the value through the lens, you get the value that was set.
2. `set(lens, b, set(lens, a, store)) ≡ set(lens, b, store)` — If you set a lens value to `a` and then immediately set the lens value to `b`, it's the same as if you'd just set the value to `b`.
3. `set(lens, view(lens, store), store) ≡ store` — If you get the lens value from the store, and then immediately set that value back into the store, the value is unchanged.

Before we dive into code examples, remember that if you're using lenses in production, you should probably be using a well tested lens library. The best one I know of in JavaScript is Ramda. We're going to skip that for now and build some naive lenses ourselves, just for the sake of learning:

```javascript
// Pure functions to view and set which can be used with any lens:
const view = (lens, store) => lens.view(store);
const set = (lens, value, store) => lens.set(value, store);

// A function which takes a prop, and returns naive
// lens accessors for that prop.
const lensProp = prop => ({
  view: store => store[prop],
  // This is very naive, because it only works for objects:
  set: (value, store) => ({
    ...store,
    [prop]: value
  })
});

// An example store object. An object you access with a lens
// is often called the "store" object:
const fooStore = {
  a: 'foo',
  b: 'bar'
};

```

[57]https://stackoverflow.com/questions/17198072/how-is-anamorphism-related-to-lens

```
23  const aLens = lensProp('a');
24  const bLens = lensProp('b');
25
26  // Destructure the `a` and `b` props from the lens using
27  // the `view()` function.
28  const a = view(aLens, fooStore);
29  const b = view(bLens, fooStore);
30  console.log(a, b); // 'foo' 'bar'
31
32  // Set a value into our store using the `aLens`:
33  const bazStore = set(aLens, 'baz', fooStore);
34
35  // View the newly set value.
36  console.log( view(aLens, bazStore) ); // 'baz'
```

Let's prove the lens laws for these functions:

```
1   const store = fooStore;
2
3   {
4     // `view(lens, set(lens, value, store))` = `value`
5     // If you set a value into the store, and immediately view the value
6     // through the lens, you get the value that was set.
7     const lens = lensProp('a');
8     const value = 'baz';
9
10    const a = value;
11    const b = view(lens, set(lens, value, store));
12
13    console.log(a, b); // 'baz' 'baz'
14  }
15
16  {
17    // set(lens, b, set(lens, a, store)) = set(lens, b, store)
18    // If you set a lens value to `a` and then immediately set the lens value to `b`,
19    // it's the same as if you'd just set the value to `b`.
20    const lens = lensProp('a');
21
22    const a = 'bar';
23    const b = 'baz';
24
25    const r1 = set(lens, b, set(lens, a, store));
26    const r2 = set(lens, b, store);
```

```
27
28    console.log(r1, r2); // {a: "baz", b: "bar"} {a: "baz", b: "bar"}
29  }
30
31  {
32    // `set(lens, view(lens, store), store)` = `store`
33    // If you get the lens value from the store, and then immediately set that value
34    // back into the store, the value is unchanged.
35    const lens = lensProp('a');
36
37    const r1 = set(lens, view(lens, store), store);
38    const r2 = store;
39
40    console.log(r1, r2); // {a: "foo", b: "bar"} {a: "foo", b: "bar"}
41  }
```

Composing Lenses

Lenses are composable. When you compose lenses, the resulting lens will dive deep into the object, traversing the full object path. Let's import the more full-featured `lensProp` from Ramda to demonstrate:

```
1   import { compose, lensProp, view } from 'ramda';
2
3   const lensProps = [
4     'foo',
5     'bar',
6     1
7   ];
8
9   const lenses = lensProps.map(lensProp);
10
11  const truth = compose(...lenses);
12
13  const obj = {
14    foo: {
15      bar: [false, true]
16    }
17  };
18
19  console.log(
```

```
20      view(truth, obj)
21    );
```

That's great, but there's more to composition with lenses that we should be aware of. Let's take a deeper dive.

Over

It's possible to apply a function from a => b in the context of any functor data type. We've already demonstrated that functor mapping *is composition*. Similarly, we can apply a function to the value of focus in a lens. Typically, that value would be of the same type, so it would be a function from a => a. The lens map operation is commonly called "over" in JavaScript libraries. We can create it like this:

```
1  // over = (lens, f: a => a, store) => store
2  const over = (lens, f, store) => set(lens, f(view(lens, store)), store);
3  const uppercase = x => x.toUpperCase();
4
5  console.log(
6    over(aLens, uppercase, store) // { a: "FOO", b: "bar" }
7  );
```

Setters mirror the functor laws:

```
1  { // if you map the identity function over a lens
2    // the store is unchanged.
3    const id = x => x;
4    const lens = aLens;
5    const a = over(lens, id, store);
6    const b = store;
7
8    console.log(a, b);
9  }
```

For the composition example, we're going to use an autocurried version of over:

```
import { curry } from 'ramda';

const over = curry(
  (lens, f, store) => set(lens, f(view(lens, store)), store)
);
```

Now it's easy to see that lenses under the over operation also obey the functor composition law:

```
{ // over(lens, f) after over(lens g) is the same as
  // over(lens, compose(f, g))
  const lens = aLens;

  const store = {
    a: 20
  };

  const g = n => n + 1;
  const f = n => n * 2;

  const a = compose(
    over(lens, f),
    over(lens, g)
  );

  const b = over(lens, compose(f, g));

  console.log(
    a(store), // {a: 42}
    b(store)  // {a: 42}
  );
}
```

We've barely scratched the surface of lenses here, but it should be enough to get you started. For a lot more, detail, Edward Kmett has spoken a lot on the topic, and many people have written much more in-depth explorations.

Transducers

Prior to taking on transducers, you should first have a strong understanding of both **reducers** and **function composition**.

> Transduce: Derived from the 17th century scientific latin, "transductionem" means "to change over, convert". It is further derived from "transducere/traducere", which means "to lead along or across, transfer".

A **transducer** is a composable **higher order reducer**. It takes a reducer as input, and returns another reducer.

Transducers are:

- Composable using simple function composition
- Efficient for large collections or infinite streams: Only enumerates over the signal once, regardless of the number of operations in the pipeline
- Able to transduce over any enumerable source (e.g., arrays, trees, streams, graphs, etc...)
- Usable for either lazy or eager evaluation with no changes to the transducer pipeline

Reducers *fold* multiple inputs into single outputs, where "fold" can be replaced with virtually any binary operation that produces a single output, such as:

```
// Sums: (1, 2) = 3
const add = (a, c) => a + c;

// Products: (2, 4) = 8
const multiply = (a, c) => a * c;

// String concatenation: ('abc', '123') = 'abc123'
const concatString = (a, c) => a + c;

// Array concatenation: ([1,2], [3,4]) = [1, 2, 3, 4]
const concatArray = (a, c) => [...a, ...c];
```

Transducers do much the same thing, but unlike ordinary reducers, transducers are composable using normal function composition. In other words, you can combine any number of transducers to form a new transducer which links each component transducer together in series.

Normal reducers can't compose, because they expect two arguments, and only return a single output value, so you can't simply connect the output to the input of the next reducer in the series. The types don't line up:

```
1  f: (a, c) => a
2  g:         (a, c) => a
3  h: ???
```

Transducers have a different signature:

```
1  f: reducer => reducer
2  g:           reducer => reducer
3  h: reducer  =>         reducer
```

Since all the functions in the pipeline accept a reducer and return a reducer, the input and output types always line up for easy composition.

Why Transducers?

Often, when we process data, it's useful to break up the processing into multiple independent, composable stages. For example, it's very common to select some data from a larger set, and then process that data. You may be tempted to do something like this:

```
1  const friends = [
2    { id: 1, name: 'Sting', nearMe: true },
3    { id: 2, name: 'Radiohead', nearMe: true },
4    { id: 3, name: 'NIN', nearMe: false },
5    { id: 4, name: 'Echo', nearMe: true },
6    { id: 5, name: 'Zeppelin', nearMe: false }
7  ];
8
9  const isNearMe = ({ nearMe }) => nearMe;
10
11 const getName = ({ name }) => name;
12
13 const results = friends
14   .filter(isNearMe)
15   .map(getName);
16
17 console.log(results);
18 // => ["Sting", "Radiohead", "Echo"]
```

This is fine for small lists like this, but there are some potential problems:

1. This only works for arrays. What about potentially infinite streams of data coming in from a network subscription, or a social graph with friends-of-friends?

2. Each time you use the dot chaining syntax on an array, JavaScript builds up a whole new intermediate array before moving onto the next operation in the chain. If you have a list of 2,000,000 "friends" to wade through, that could slow things down by an order of magnitude or two. With transducers, you can stream each friend through the complete pipeline without building up intermediate collections between them, saving lots of time and memory churn.
3. With dot chaining, you have to build different implementations of standard operations, like `.filter()`, `.map()`, `.reduce()`, `.concat()`, and so on. The array methods are built into JavaScript, but what if you want to build a custom data type and support a bunch of standard operations without writing them all from scratch? Transducers can potentially work with any transport data type: Write an operator once, use it anywhere that supports transducers.

Let's see what this would look like with transducers. This code won't work yet, but follow along, and you'll be able to build every piece of this transducer pipeline yourself:

```javascript
const friends = [
  { id: 1, name: 'Sting', nearMe: true },
  { id: 2, name: 'Radiohead', nearMe: true },
  { id: 3, name: 'NIN', nearMe: false },
  { id: 4, name: 'Echo', nearMe: true },
  { id: 5, name: 'Zeppelin', nearMe: false }
];

const isNearMe = ({ nearMe }) => nearMe;

const getName = ({ name }) => name;

const getFriendsNearMe = compose(
  filter(isNearMe),
  map(getName)
);

const results2 = toArray(getFriendsNearMe, friends);
```

Transducers don't do anything until you tell them to start and feed them some data to process, which is why we need `toArray()`. It supplies the transducable process and tells the transducer to transduce the results into a new array. You could tell it to transduce to a stream, or an observable, or anything you like, instead of calling `toArray()`.

A transducer could map numbers to strings, or objects to arrays, or arrays to smaller arrays, or not change anything at all, mapping `{ x, y, z }` -> `{ x, y, z }`. Transducers may also filter parts of the signal out of the stream `{ x, y, z }` -> `{ x, y }`, or even generate new values to insert into the output stream, `{ x, y, z }` -> `{ x, xx, y, yy, z, zz }`.

I will use the words "signal" and "stream" somewhat interchangeably in this section. Keep in mind when I say "stream", I'm not referring to any specific data type: simply a sequence of zero or more values, or *a list of values expressed over time.*

Background and Etymology

In hardware signal processing systems, a transducer is a device which converts one form of energy to another, e.g., audio waves to electrical, as in a microphone transducer. In other words, it transforms one kind of signal into another kind of signal. Likewise, a transducer in code converts from one signal to another signal.

Use of the word "transducers" and the general concept of composable pipelines of data transformations in software date back at least to the 1960s, but our ideas about how they should work have changed from one language and context to the next. Many software engineers in the early days of computer science were also electrical engineers. The general study of computer science in those days often dealt both with hardware and software design. Hence, thinking of computational processes as "transducers" was not particularly novel. It's possible to encounter the term in early computer science literature — particularly in the context of Digital Signal Processing (DSP) and **data flow programming**.

In the 1960s, groundbreaking work was happening in graphical computing in MIT's Lincoln Laboratory using the TX-2 computer system, a precursor to the US Air Force SAGE defense system. Ivan Sutherland's famous Sketchpad[58], developed in 1961-1962, was an early example of object prototype delegation and graphical programming using a light pen.

Ivan's brother, William Robert "Bert" Sutherland was one of several pioneers in data flow programming. He built a data flow programming environment on top of Sketchpad, which described software "procedures" as directed graphs of operator nodes with outputs linked to the inputs of other nodes. He wrote about the experience in his 1966 paper, "The On-Line Graphical Specification of Computer Procedures"[59]. Instead of arrays and array processing, everything is represented as a stream of values in a continuously running, interactive program loop. Each value is processed by each node as it arrives at the parameter input. You can find similar systems today in Unreal Engine's Blueprints Visual Scripting Environment[60] or Native Instruments' Reaktor[61], a visual programming environment used by musicians to build custom audio synthesizers.

---

[58]https://dspace.mit.edu/handle/1721.1/14979
[59]https://dspace.mit.edu/handle/1721.1/13474
[60]https://docs.unrealengine.com/en-us/Engine/Blueprints
[61]https://www.native-instruments.com/en/products/komplete/synths/reaktor-6/

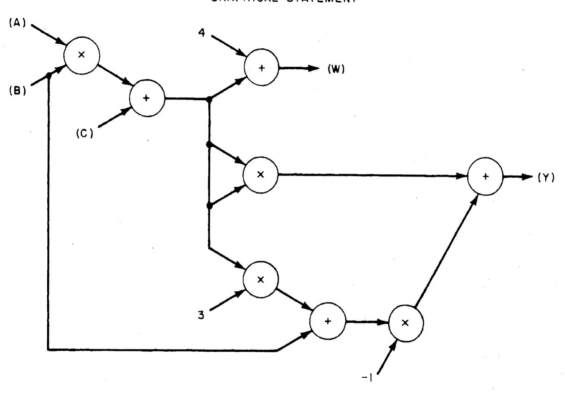

Pipeline of connected graphical operators from Bert Sutherland's paper

As far as I'm aware, the first book to popularize the term "transducer" in the context of general purpose software-based stream processing was the 1985 MIT text book for a computer science course called "Structure and Interpretation of Computer Programs"[62] (**SICP**) by Harold Abelson and Gerald Jay Sussman, with Julie Sussman. However, the use of the term "transducer" in the context of digital signal processing predates SICP.

> **Note:** SICP is still an excellent introduction to computer science coming from a functional programming perspective. It remains my favorite book on the topic.

More recently, transducers have been independently rediscovered and a *different protocol* developed for Clojure by Rich Hickey (circa 2014), who is famous for carefully selecting words for concepts

---

[62]https://www.amazon.com/Structure-Interpretation-Computer-Programs-Engineering/dp/0262510871/ref=as_li_ss_tl?ie=UTF8&qid=1507159222&sr=8-1&keywords=sicp&linkCode=ll1&tag=eejs-20&linkId=44b40411506b45f32abf1b70b44574d2

based on etymology. In this case, I'd say he nailed it, because Clojure transducers fill almost exactly the same niche as transducers in SICP, and they share many common characteristics. However, they are *not strictly the same thing.*

Transducers as a general concept (not specifically Hickey's protocol specification) have had considerable impact on important branches of computer science including data flow programming, signal processing for scientific and media applications, networking, artificial intelligence, etc. As we develop better tools and techniques to express transducers in our application code, they are beginning to help us make better sense of every kind of software composition, including user interface behaviors in web and mobile apps, and in the future, could also serve us well to help manage the complexity of augmented reality, autonomous devices and vehicles, etc.

For the purpose of this discussion, when I say "transducer", I'm not referring to SICP transducers, though it may sound like I'm describing them if you're already familiar with transducers from SICP. I'm also not referring *specifically* to Clojure's transducers, or the transducer protocol that has become a de facto standard in JavaScript (supported by Ramda, Transducers-JS, RxJS, etc...). I'm referring to the *general concept of a higher-order reducer* — a transformation of a transformation.

In my view, the particular details of the transducer protocols matter a whole lot less than the general principles and underlying mathematical properties of transducers, however, if you want to use transducers in production, my current recommendation is to use an existing library which implements the transducers protocol for interoperability reasons.

The transducers that I will describe here should be considered pseudo-code to express the concepts. They are *not compatible with the transducer protocol*, and *should not be used in production*. If you want to learn how to use a particular library's transducers, refer to the library documentation. I'm writing them this way to lift up the hood and let you see how they work without forcing you to learn the protocol at the same time.

When we're done, you should have a better understanding of transducers in general, and how you might apply them in any context, with any library, in any language that supports closures and higher-order functions.

A Musical Analogy for Transducers

If you're among the large number of software developers who are also musicians, a music analogy may be useful: You can think of transducers like signal processing gear (e.g., guitar distortion pedals, EQ, volume knobs, echo, reverb, and audio mixers).

To record a song using musical instruments, we need some sort of physical transducer (i.e., a microphone) to convert the sound waves in the air into electricity on the wire. Then we need to route that wire to whatever signal processing units we'd like to use. For example, adding distortion to an electric guitar, or reverb to a voice track. Eventually this collection of different sounds must be aggregated together and mixed to form a single signal (or collection of channels) representing the final recording.

In other words, the signal flow might look something like this. Imagine the arrows are wires between transducers:

```
[ Source ] -> [ Mic ] -> [ Filter ] -> [ Mixer ] -> [ Recording ]
```

In more general terms, you could express it like this:

```
[ Enumerator ] -> [ Transducer ] -> [ Transducer ] -> [ Accumulator ]
```

If you've ever used music production software, this might remind you of a chain of audio effects. That's a good intuition to have when you're thinking about transducers, but they can be applied much more generally to numbers, objects, animation frames, 3d models, or anything else you can represent in software.

Renoise music software effects pipeline

You may be experienced with something that behaves a little bit like a transducer if you've ever used the map method on arrays. For example, to double a series of numbers:

```
const double = x => x * 2;
const arr = [1, 2, 3];

const result = arr.map(double);
```

In this example, the array is an enumerable object. The map method enumerates over the original array, and passes its elements through the processing stage, `double`, which multiplies each element by 2, then accumulates the results into a new array.

You can even compose effects like this:

```
const double = x => x * 2;
const isEven = x => x % 2 === 0;

const arr = [1, 2, 3, 4, 5, 6];

const result = arr
  .filter(isEven)
  .map(double)
;

console.log(result);
// [4, 8, 12]
```

But what if you want to filter and double a potentially infinite stream of numbers, such as a drone's telemetry data?

Arrays can't be infinite, and each stage in the array processing requires you to process the entire array before a single value can flow through the next stage in the pipeline. That same limitation means that composition using array methods will have degraded performance because a new array will need to be created and a new collection iterated over for each stage in the composition.

Imagine you have two sections of tubing, each of which represents a transformation to be applied to the data stream, and a string representing the stream. The first transformation represents the isEven filter, and the next represents the double map. In order to produce a single fully transformed value from an array, you'd have to run the entire string through the first tube first, resulting in a completely new, filtered array *before* you can process even a single value through the double tube. When you finally do get to double your first value, you have to wait for the entire array to be doubled before you can read a single result.

So, the code above is equivalent to this:

```
const double = x => x * 2;
const isEven = x => x % 2 === 0;

const arr = [1, 2, 3, 4, 5, 6];

const tempResult = arr.filter(isEven);
const result = tempResult.map(double);

console.log(result);
// [4, 8, 12]
```

The alternative is to flow a value directly from the filtered output to the mapping transformation without creating and iterating over a new, temporary array in between. Flowing the values through one at a time removes the need to iterate over the same collection for each stage in the transducing process, and transducers can signal a stop at any time, meaning you don't need to enumerate each stage deeper over the collection than required to produce the desired values.

There are two ways to do that:

- **Pull**: lazy evaluation, or
- **Push**: eager evaluation

A pull API waits until a consumer asks for the next value. A good example in JavaScript is an Iterable, such as the object produced by a generator function. Nothing happens in the generator function until you ask for the next value by calling .next() on the iterator object it returns.

A push API enumerates over the source values and pushes them through the tubes as fast as it can. A call to array.reduce() is a good example of a push API. array.reduce() takes one value at a time from the array and pushes it through the reducer, resulting in a new value at the other end. For eager processes like array reduce, the process is immediately repeated for each element in the array until the entire array has been processed, blocking further program execution in the meantime.

Transducers don't care whether you pull or push. Transducers have no awareness of the data structure they're acting on. They simply call the reducer you pass into them to accumulate new values.

Transducers are **higher order reducers**: Reducer functions that take a reducer and return a new reducer. Rich Hickey describes transducers as **process transformations**, meaning that as opposed to simply changing the values flowing through transducers, transducers change the processes that act on those values.

The signatures look like this:

```
reducer = (accumulator, current) => accumulator

transducer = reducer => reducer
```

Or, to spell it out:

```
transducer = ((accumulator, current) => accumulator) =>
  ((accumulator, current) => accumulator)
```

Generally speaking though, most transducers will need to be partially applied to some arguments to specialize them. For example, a map transducer might look like this:

```
map = transform => reducer => reducer
```

Or more specifically:

```
map = (a => b) => step => reducer
```

In other words, a map transducer takes a mapping function (called a transform) and a reducer (called the `step` function), and returns a new reducer. The `step` function is a reducer to call when we've produced a new value to add to the accumulator in the next step.

Let's look at some naive examples:

```javascript
const compose = (...fns) => x => fns.reduceRight((y, f) => f(y), x);

const map = f => step =>
  (a, c) => step(a, f(c));

const filter = predicate => step =>
  (a, c) => predicate(c) ? step(a, c) : a;

const isEven = n => n % 2 === 0;
const double = n => n * 2;

const doubleEvens = compose(
  filter(isEven),
  map(double)
);

const arrayConcat = (a, c) => a.concat([c]);

const xform = doubleEvens(arrayConcat);

const result = [1,2,3,4,5,6].reduce(xform, []); // [4, 8, 12]

console.log(result);
```

That's a lot to absorb. Let's break it down. `map` applies a function to the values inside some context. In this case, the context is the transducer pipeline. It looks roughly like this:

```javascript
const map = f => step =>
  (a, c) => step(a, f(c));
```

You can use it like this:

```javascript
const double = x => x * 2;

const doubleMap = map(double);

const step = (a, c) => console.log(c);

doubleMap(step)(0, 4);  // 8
doubleMap(step)(0, 21); // 42
```

The zeros in the function calls at the end represent the initial values for the reducers. Note that the step function is supposed to be a reducer, but for demonstration purposes, we can hijack it and log to the console. You can use the same trick in your unit tests if you need to make assertions about how the step function gets used.

Transducers get interesting when we compose them together. Let's implement a simplified filter transducer:

```
const filter = predicate => step =>
  (a, c) => predicate(c) ? step(a, c) : a;
```

Filter takes a predicate function and only passes through the values that match the predicate. Otherwise, the returned reducer returns the accumulator, unchanged.

Since both of these functions take a reducer and return a reducer, we can compose them with simple function composition:

```
const compose = (...fns) => x => fns.reduceRight((y, f) => f(y), x);

const isEven = n => n % 2 === 0;
const double = n => n * 2;

const doubleEvens = compose(
  filter(isEven),
  map(double)
);
```

This will also return a transducer, which means we must supply a final step function in order to tell the transducer how to accumulate the result:

```
const arrayConcat = (a, c) => a.concat([c]);

const xform = doubleEvens(arrayConcat);
```

The result of this call is a standard reducer that we can pass directly to any compatible reduce API. The second argument represents the initial value of the reduction. In this case, an empty array:

```
const result = [1,2,3,4,5,6].reduce(xform, []); // [4, 8, 12]
```

If this seems like a lot of work, keep in mind there are already functional programming libraries that supply common transducers along with utilities such as `compose`, which handles function composition, and `into`, which transduces a value into the given empty value, e.g.:

```
1  const xform = compose(
2    map(inc),
3    filter(isEven)
4  );
5
6  into([], xform, [1,2,3,4]); // [2, 4]
```

With most of the required tools already in the tool belt, programming with transducers is really intuitive.

Some popular libraries which support transducers include Ramda, RxJS, and Mori.

Transducers compose top-to-bottom.

Transducers under standard function composition (f(g(x))) apply top to bottom/left-to-right rather than bottom-to-top/right-to-left. In other words, using normal function composition, compose(f, g) means "compose f *after* g". Transducers wrap around other transducers under composition. In other words, a transducer says "I'm going to do my thing, and *then* call the next transducer in the pipeline", which has the effect of turning the execution stack inside out.

Imagine you have a stack of papers, the top labeled, f, the next, g, and the next h. For each sheet, take the sheet off the top of the stack and place it onto the top of a new adjacent stack. When you're done, you'll have a stack whose sheets are labeled h, then g, then f.

Transducer Rules

The examples above are naive because they ignore the rules that transducers must follow for interoperability.

As with most things in software, transducers and transducing processes need to obey some rules:

1. **Initialization**: Given no initial accumulator value, a transducer must call the step function to produce a valid initial value to act on. The value should represent the empty state. For example, an accumulator that accumulates an array should supply an empty array when its step function is called with no arguments.
2. **Early termination**: A process that uses transducers must check for and stop when it receives a reduced accumulator value. Additionally, a transducer step function that uses a nested reduce must check for and convey reduced values when they are encountered.
3. **Completion (optional)**: Some transducing processes never complete, but those that do should call the completion function to produce a final value and/or flush state, and stateful transducers should supply a completion operation that cleans up any accumulated resources and potentially produces one final value.

Initialization

Let's go back to the `map` operation and make sure that it obeys the initialization (empty) law. Of course, we don't need to do anything special, just pass the request down the pipeline using the step function to create a default value:

```
const map = f => step => (a = step(), c) => (
  step(a, f(c))
);
```

The part we care about is `a = step()` in the function signature. If there is no value for `a` (the accumulator), we'll create one by asking the next reducer in the chain to produce it. Eventually, it will reach the end of the pipeline and (hopefully) create a valid initial value for us.

Remember this rule: When called with no arguments, a reducer should always return a valid initial (empty) value for the reduction. It's generally a good idea to obey this rule for any reducer function, including reducers for React or Redux.

Early Termination

It's possible to signal to other transducers in the pipeline that we're done reducing, and they should not expect to process any more values. Upon seeing a `reduced` value, other transducers may decide to stop adding to the collection, and the transducing process (as controlled by the final `step()` function) may decide to stop enumerating over values. The transducing process may make one more call as a result of receiving a `reduced` value: The completion call mentioned above. We can signal that intention with a special **reduced** accumulator value.

What is a reduced value? It could be as simple as wrapping the accumulator value in a special type called `reduced`. Think of it like wrapping a package in a box and labelling the box with messages like "Express" or "Fragile". Metadata wrappers like this are common in computing. For example: http messages are wrapped in containers called "request" or "response", and those container types have headers that supply information like status codes, expected message length, authorization parameters, etc...

Basically, it's a way of sending multiple messages where only a single value is expected. A minimal (non-standard) example of a `reduced()` type lift might look like this:

```javascript
const reduced = v => ({
  get isReduced () {
    return true;
  },
  valueOf: () => v,
  toString: () => `Reduced(${ JSON.stringify(v) })`
});
```

The only parts that are strictly required are:

- **The type lift**: A way to get the value inside the type (e.g., the `reduced` function, in this case)
- **Type identification**: A way to test the value to see if it is a value of `reduced` (e.g., the `isReduced` getter)
- **Value extraction**: A way to get the value back out of the type (e.g., `valueOf()`)

`toString()` is included here strictly for debugging convenience. It lets you introspect both the type and the value at the same time in the console.

Completion

> "In the completion step, a transducer with reduction state should flush state prior to calling the nested transformer's completion function, unless it has previously seen a reduced value from the nested step in which case pending state should be discarded." ~ Clojure transducers documentation

In other words, if you have more state to flush after the previous function has signaled that it's finished reducing, the completion step is the time to handle it. At this stage, you can optionally:

- Send one more value (flush your pending state)
- Discard your pending state
- Perform any required state cleanup

Transducing

It's possible to transduce over lots of different types of data, but the process can be generalized:

```javascript
// import a standard curry, or use this magic spell:
const curry = (
  f, arr = []
) => (...args) => (
  a => a.length === f.length ?
    f(...a) :
    curry(f, a)
)([...arr, ...args]);

const transduce = curry((step, initial, xform, foldable) =>
  foldable.reduce(xform(step), initial)
);
```

The `transduce()` function takes a step function (the final step in the transducer pipeline), an initial value for the accumulator, a transducer, and a foldable. A **foldable** is any object that supplies a `.reduce()` method.

With `transduce()` defined, we can easily create a function that transduces to an array. First, we need a reducer that reduces to an array:

```javascript
const concatArray = (a, c) => a.concat([c]);
```

Now we can use the curried `transduce()` to create a partial application that transduces to arrays:

```javascript
const toArray = transduce(concatArray, []);
```

With `toArray()` we can replace two lines of code with one, and reuse it in a lot of other situations, besides:

```javascript
// Manual transduce:
const xform = doubleEvens(arrayConcat);
const result = [1,2,3,4,5,6].reduce(xform, []);
// => [4, 8, 12]
```

```javascript
// Automatic transduce:
const result2 = toArray(doubleEvens, [1,2,3,4,5,6]);
console.log(result2); // [4, 8, 12]
```

The Transducer Protocol

Up to this point, I've been hiding some details behind a curtain, but it's time to take a look at them now. Transducers are not really a single function. They're made from 3 different functions. Clojure switches between them using pattern matching on the function's arity.

In computer science, the **arity** of a function is the number of arguments a function takes. In the case of transducers, there are two arguments to the reducer function, the accumulator and the current value. In Clojure, Both are *optional*, and the behavior changes based on whether or not the arguments get passed. If a parameter is not passed, the type of that parameter inside the function is `undefined`.

The JavaScript transducer protocol handles things a little differently. Instead of using function arity, JavaScript transducers are a function that take a transducer and return a transducer. The transducer is an object with three methods:

- **init** Return a valid initial value for the accumulator (usually, just call the next `step()`).
- **step** Apply the transform, e.g., for `map(f)`: `step(accumulator, f(current))`.
- **result** If a transducer is called without a new value, it should handle its completion step (usually `step(a)`, unless the transducer is stateful).

  Note: The transducer protocol in JavaScript uses @@transducer/init, @@transducer/step, and @@transducer/result, respectively.

Here is a less naive implementation of the map transducer:

```
const map = f => next => transducer({
  init: () => next.init(),
  result: a => next.result(a),
  step: (a, c) => next.step(a, f(c))
});
```

By default, most transducers should pass the `init()` call to the next transducer in the pipeline, because we don't know the transport data type, so we can't produce a valid initial value for it.

Additionally, the special `reduced` object uses these properties (also namespaced `@@transducer/<name>` in the transducer protocol:

- **reduced** A boolean value that is always `true` for reduced values.
- **value** The reduced value.

Conclusion

Transducers are composable higher order reducers which can reduce over any underlying data type.

Transducers produce code that can be orders of magnitude more efficient than dot chaining with arrays, and handle potentially infinite data sets without creating intermediate aggregations.

> **Note:** Transducers aren't *always* faster than built-in array methods. The performance benefits tend to kick in when the data set is very large (hundreds of thousands of items), or pipelines are quite large (adding significantly to the number of iterations required using method chains). If you're after the performance benefits, remember to profile.

Take another look at the example from the introduction. You should be able to build `filter()`, `map()`, and `toArray()` using the example code as a reference and make this code work:

```javascript
const friends = [
  { id: 1, name: 'Sting', nearMe: true },
  { id: 2, name: 'Radiohead', nearMe: true },
  { id: 3, name: 'NIN', nearMe: false },
  { id: 4, name: 'Echo', nearMe: true },
  { id: 5, name: 'Zeppelin', nearMe: false }
];

const isNearMe = ({ nearMe }) => nearMe;

const getName = ({ name }) => name;

const getFriendsNearMe = compose(
  filter(isNearMe),
  map(getName)
);

const results2 = toArray(getFriendsNearMe, friends);
```

In production, you can use transducers from Ramda[63], RxJS[64], transducers-js[65], or Mori[66].

All of those work a little differently than the example code here, but follow all the same fundamental principles.

Here's an example from Ramda:

---

[63] http://ramdajs.com/
[64] https://github.com/ReactiveX/rxjs
[65] https://github.com/cognitect-labs/transducers-js
[66] https://github.com/swannodette/mori

```javascript
import {
  compose,
  filter,
  map,
  into
} from 'ramda';

const isEven = n => n % 2 === 0;
const double = n => n * 2;

const doubleEvens = compose(
  filter(isEven),
  map(double)
);

const arr = [1, 2, 3, 4, 5, 6];

// into = (structure, transducer, data) => result
// into transduces the data using the supplied
// transducer into the structure passed as the
// first argument.
const result = into([], doubleEvens, arr);

console.log(result); // [4, 8, 12]
```

Whenever I need to combine a number of operations, such as `map`, `filter`, `chunk`, `take`, and so on, I reach for transducers to optimize the process and keep the code readable and clean. Give them a try.

Elements of JavaScript Style

In 1920, "The Elements of Style" by William Strunk Jr. was published, which set guidelines for English language style that have lasted the test of time. You can improve your code by applying similar standards to your code style.

The following are guidelines, not immutable laws. There may be valid reasons to deviate from them if doing so clarifies the meaning of the code, but be vigilant and self-aware. These guidelines have stood the test of time for good reason: They're usually right. Deviate from them only for good reason—not simply on a whim or a personal style preference.

Almost every guideline from the elementary principles of composition applies to source code:

- Make the paragraph the unit of composition: One paragraph to each topic.
- Omit needless words.
- Use active voice.
- Avoid a succession of loose sentences.
- Keep related words together.
- Put statements in positive form.
- Use parallel construction on parallel concepts.

We can apply nearly identical concepts to code style:

1. Make the function the unit of composition. One job for each function.
2. Omit needless code.
3. Use active voice.
4. Avoid a succession of loose statements.
5. Keep related code together.
6. Put statements and expressions in positive form.
7. Use parallel code for parallel concepts.

1. Make the function the unit of composition. One job for each function.

> The essence of software development is composition. We build software by composing modules, functions, and data structures together.
>
> Understanding how to write and compose functions is a fundamental skill for software developers.

Modules are simply collections of one or more functions or data structures, and data structures are how we represent program state, but nothing interesting happens until we apply a function.

In JavaScript, there are three kinds of functions:

- Communicating functions: Functions which perform I/O.
- Procedural functions: A list of instructions, grouped together.
- Mapping functions: Given some input, return some corresponding output.

While all useful programs need I/O, and many programs follow some procedural sequences, the majority of your functions should be mapping functions: Given some input, the function will return some corresponding output.

One job for each function: If your function is for I/O, don't mix that I/O with mapping (calculation). If your function is for mapping, don't mix it with I/O. By definition, procedural functions violate this guideline. Procedural functions also violate another guideline: Avoid a succession of loose statements.

The ideal function is a simple, deterministic, pure function:

- Given the same input, always return the same output
- No side-effects

See also, "Pure Functions".

2. Omit needless code.

> "Vigorous writing is concise. A sentence should contain no unnecessary words, a paragraph no unnecessary sentences, for the same reason that a drawing should have no unnecessary lines and a machine no unnecessary parts. This requires not that the writer make all sentences short, or avoid all detail and treat subjects only in outline, but that every word tell." [Needless words omitted.]
>
> ~ William Strunk, Jr., The Elements of Style

Concise code is critical in software because more code creates more surface area for bugs to hide in. *Less code = fewer places for bugs to hide = fewer bugs.*

Concise code is more legible because it has a higher signal-to-noise ratio: The reader must sift through less syntax noise to reach the meaning. *Less code = less syntax noise = stronger signal for meaning transmission.*

To borrow a word from The Elements of Style: Concise code is more vigorous.

```
1  function secret (message) {
2    return function () {
3      return message;
4    }
5  };
```

Can be reduced to:

```
1  const secret = msg => () => msg;
```

This is much more readable to those familiar with concise arrow functions (introduced in 2015 with ES6). It omits unnecessary syntax: Braces, the `function` keyword, and the `return` statement.

The first includes unnecessary syntax. Braces, the `function` keyword, and the `return` statement serve no purpose to those familiar with concise arrow syntax. It exists only to make the code familiar to those who are not yet fluent with ES6.

ES6 has been the language standard since 2015. It's time to get familiar.

Omit needless variables.

Sometimes we're tempted to assign names to things that don't really need to be named. The problem is that the human brain has a limited number of resources available in working memory, and each variable must be stored as a discrete quanta, occupying one of the available working memory slots.

For this reason, experienced developers learn to eliminate variables that don't need to exist.

For example, in most situations, you should omit variables created only to name return values. The name of your function should provide adequate information about what the function will return. Consider the following:

```
1  const getFullName = ({firstName, lastName}) => {
2    const fullName = firstName + ' ' + lastName;
3    return fullName;
4  };
```

vs…

```
1  const getFullName = ({firstName, lastName}) => (
2    firstName + ' ' + lastName
3  );
```

Another common way developers can reduce variables is to take advantage of function composition and point-free style.

Point-free style is a way of defining functions without referencing the arguments on which the functions operate. Common ways of achieving point-free style include currying and function composition.

Let's look at an example using curry:

```
const add2 = a => b => a + b;

// Now we can define a point-free inc()
// that adds 1 to any number.
const inc = add2(1);

inc(3); // 4
```

Take a look at the definition of the `inc()` function. Notice that it doesn't use the `function` keyword, or the fat arrow syntax (=>). There's no place to list parameters, because the function doesn't make use of a parameter list internally. Instead, it returns a function that knows how to deal with the arguments.

Let's look at another example using function composition. Function composition is the process of applying a function to the result of another function application.

Whether you realize it or not, you use function composition all the time. You use it whenever you chain methods like `.map()` or `promise.then()`, for example. In it's most basic form, it looks like this: `f(g(x))`. In algebra this composition is usually written $f \circ g$ (often pronounced, "f *after* g" or "f *composed with* g").

When you compose two functions together, you eliminate the need to create a variable to hold the intermediary value between the two function applications. Let's see how function composition can clean up some code:

```
const g = n => n + 1;
const f = n => n * 2;

// With points:
const incThenDoublePoints = n => {
  const incremented = g(n);
  return f(incremented);
};

incThenDoublePoints(20); // 42
```

vs...

```
const g = n => n + 1;
const f = n => n * 2;

// compose2 - Take two functions and return their composition
const compose2 = (f, g) => x => f(g(x));


// Point-free:
const incThenDoublePointFree = compose2(f, g);

incThenDoublePointFree(20); // 42
```

You can do the same thing with any functor. A *functor* is anything you can map over, e.g., arrays (`array.map()`) or promises (`promise.then()`).

Let's write another version of `compose2()` using `.map()` chaining for function composition:

```
const compose2 = (f, g) => x => [x].map(g).map(f).pop();

const incThenDoublePointFree = compose2(f, g);

incThenDoublePointFree(20); // 42
```

You're doing much the same thing every time you use promise chains.

Virtually every functional programming library has at least two versions of compose utilities: `compose()`, which applies functions right-to-left, and `pipe()`, which applies functions left-to-right.

Lodash calls them `compose()` and `flow()`. When I use them from Lodash, I always import it like this:

```
import pipe from 'lodash/fp/flow';
pipe(g, f)(20); // 42
```

However, this isn't much more code, and it does the same thing:

```
const pipe = (...fns) => x => fns.reduce((acc, fn) => fn(acc), x);
pipe(g, f)(20); // 42
```

If this function composition stuff sounds alien to you, and you're not sure how you'd use it, give this careful thought:

> The essence of software development is composition. We build applications by composing smaller modules, functions, and data structures.

From that you can conclude that understanding the tools of function and object composition are as fundamental as a home builder understanding drills and nail guns.

When you use imperative code to piece together functions with intermediary variables, that's like composing those pieces with duct tape and crazy glue.

Remember:

- If you can say the same thing with less code, without changing or obfuscating the meaning, you should.
- If you can say the same thing with fewer variables, without changing or obfuscating the meaning, you should.

3. Use active voice.

> "The active voice is usually more direct and vigorous than the passive." ~ William Strunk, Jr., The Elements of Style

Name things as directly as possible:

- `myFunction.wasCalled()` is better than `myFunction.hasBeenCalled()`
- `createUser()` is better than `User.create()`
- `notify()` is better than `Notifier.doNotification()`

Name predicates and booleans as if they are yes or no questions:

- `isActive(user)` is better than `getActiveStatus(user)`
- `isFirstRun = false;` is better than `firstRun = false;`

Name functions using verb forms:

- `increment()` is better than `plusOne()`
- `unzip()` is better than `filesFromZip()`
- `filter(isActive, array)` is better than `activeItemsFromArray(isActive, array)`

Event Handlers

Event handlers and lifecycle methods are an exception to the verb rule because they're used as qualifiers; instead of expressing what to do, they express when to do it. They should be named so that they read, "<when to act>, <verb>".

- `element.onClick(handleClick)` is better than `element.click(handleClick)`
- `component.onDragStart(handleDragStart)` is better than `component.startDrag(handleDragStart)`

In the second forms, it looks like we're trying to trigger the event, rather than respond to it.

Lifecycle Methods

Consider the following alternatives for a component hypothetical lifecycle method which exists to call a handler function before a component updates:

- componentWillBeUpdated(doSomething)
- componentWillUpdate(doSomething)
- beforeUpdate(doSomething)

The first example uses passive voice (`willBeUpdated` instead of `willUpdate`). It is a mouthful, and not any more clear than the other alternatives.

The second example is much better, but the whole point of this lifecycle method is to call a handler. `componentWillUpdate(handler)` reads as if it will update the handler, but that's not what we mean. We mean, "before the component updates, call the handler". `beforeComponentUpdate()` expresses the intention more clearly.

We can simplify even further. Since these are methods, the subject (the component) is built-in. Referring to it in the method name is redundant. Think about how it would read if you called these methods directly: `component.componentWillUpdate()`. That's like saying, "Jimmy Jimmy will have steak for dinner." You don't need to hear the subject's name twice.

```
component.beforeUpdate(doSomething)
```

Is better than:

```
component.beforeComponentUpdate(doSomething)
```

Functional mixins are functions that add properties and methods to an object. The functions are applied one after the other in an pipeline—like an assembly line. Each functional mixin takes the instance as an input, and tacks some stuff onto it before passing it on to the next function in the pipeline.

I like to name functional mixins using adjectives. You can often use "ing" or "able" suffixes to find useful adjectives. Examples:

- const duck = composeMixins(flying, quacking);
- const box = composeMixins(iterable, mappable);

4. Avoid a succession of loose statements.

> "...a series soon becomes monotonous and tedious." ~ William Strunk, Jr., The Elements of Style

Developers frequently string together sequences of events in a procedure; a group of loosely related statements designed to run one after the other. An excess of procedures is a recipe for spaghetti code.

Such sequences are frequently repeated by many similar forms, each of them subtly and sometimes unexpectedly divergent. For example, a user interface component shares the same core needs with virtually all other user interface components. Its concerns can be broken up into lifecycle stages and managed by separate functions.

Consider the following sequence:

```javascript
const drawUserProfile = ({ userId }) => {
  const userData = loadUserData(userId);
  const dataToDisplay = calculateDisplayData(userData);
  renderProfileData(dataToDisplay);
};
```

This function is really handling three different things: loading data, calculating view state from loaded data, and rendering.

In most modern front-end application architectures, each of these concerns is considered separately. By separating these concerns, we can easily mix and match different functions for each concern. For example, we could replace the renderer completely, and it would not impact the other parts of the program, e.g., React's wealth of custom renderers: React Native for native iOS & Android apps, AFrame for WebVR, ReactDOM/Server for server-side rendering, etc...

Another problem with this function is that you can't simply calculate the data to be displayed and generate the markup without first loading the data. What if you've already loaded the data? You end up doing work that you didn't need to do in subsequent calls.

Separating the concerns also makes them independently testable. I like to unit test my applications and display test results with each change as I'm writing the code. However, if we're tying render code to data loading code, I can't simply pass some fake data to the rendering code for testing purposes. I have to test the whole component end-to-end—a process which can be time consuming due to browser loading, asynchronous network I/O, etc... I won't get immediate feedback from my unit tests. Separating the functions allows you to test units in isolation from each other.

This example already has separate functions which we can feed to different lifecycle hooks in the application. Loading can be triggered when the component is mounted by the application. Calculating & rendering can happen in response to view state updates.

The result is software with responsibilities more clearly delineated: Each component can reuse the same structure and lifecycle hooks, and the software performs better; we don't repeat work that doesn't need to be repeated in subsequent cycles.

5. Keep related code together.

Many frameworks and boilerplates prescribe a method of program organization where files are grouped by technical type. This is fine if you're building a small calculator or To Do app, but for larger projects, it's usually better to group files together by feature.

For example, consider two alternative file hierarchies for a To Do app by type and feature.

Grouped by type:

```
1  .
2  ├── components
3  │   ├── todos
4  │   └── user
5  ├── reducers
6  │   ├── todos
7  │   └── user
8  └── tests
9      ├── todos
10     └── user
```

Grouped by feature:

```
1  .
2  ├── todos
3  │   ├── component
4  │   ├── reducer
5  │   └── test
6  └── user
7      ├── component
8      ├── reducer
9      └── test
```

When you group files together by feature, you avoid scrolling up and down in your file list to find all the files you need to edit to get a single feature working.

Colocate files related by feature.

6. Put statements and expressions in positive form.

> "Make definite assertions. Avoid tame, colorless, hesitating, non-committal language. Use the word not as a means of denial or in antithesis, never as a means of evasion." ~ William Strunk, Jr., The Elements of Style

- `isFlying` is better than `isNotFlying`
- `late` is better than `notOnTime`

If Statements

```
if (err) return reject(err);
// do something...
```

...is better than:

```
if (!err) {
  // ... do something
} else {
  return reject(err);
}
```

Ternaries

```
{
  [Symbol.iterator]: iterator ? iterator : defaultIterator
}
```

...is better than:

```
{
  [Symbol.iterator]: (!iterator) ? defaultIterator : iterator
}
```

Prefer strong negative statements.

Sometimes we only care about a variable if it's missing, so using a positive name would force us to negate it with the `!` operator. In those cases, prefer a strong negative form. The word "not" and the `!` operator create weak expressions.

- `if (missingValue)` is better than `if (!hasValue)`
- `if (anonymous)` is better than `if (!user)`
- `if (isEmpty(thing))` is better than `if (notDefined(thing))`

Avoid `null` and `undefined` arguments in function calls.

Don't require function callers to pass `undefined` or `null` in place of an optional parameter. Prefer named options objects instead:

```
const createEvent = ({
  title = 'Untitled',
  timeStamp = Date.now(),
  description = ''
}) => ({ title, description, timeStamp });

// later...
const birthdayParty = createEvent({
  title: 'Birthday Party',
  description: 'Best party ever!'
});
```

...is better than:

```
const createEvent = (
  title = 'Untitled',
  timeStamp = Date.now(),
  description = ''
) => ({ title, description, timeStamp });

// later...
const birthdayParty = createEvent(
  'Birthday Party',
  undefined, // This was avoidable
  'Best party ever!'
);
```

7. Use parallel code for parallel concepts.

> "...parallel construction requires that expressions of similar content and function should be outwardly similar. The likeness of form enables the reader to recognize more readily the likeness of content and function." ~ William Strunk, Jr., The Elements of Style

There are few problems in applications that have not been solved before. We end up doing the same things over and over again. When that happens, it's an opportunity for abstraction. Identify the parts that are the same, and build an abstraction that allows you to supply only the parts that are different. This is exactly what libraries and frameworks do for us.

UI components are a great example. Less than a decade ago, it was common to mingle UI updates using jQuery with application logic and network I/O. Then people began to realize that we could apply MVC to web apps on the client-side, and people began to separate models from UI update logic.

Eventually, web apps landed on a component model approach, which lets us declaratively model our components using things like JSX or HTML templates.

What we ended up with is a way of expressing UI update logic the same way for every component, rather than different imperative code for each one.

For those familiar with components, it's pretty easy to see how each component works: There's some declarative markup expressing the UI elements, event handlers for hooking up behaviors, and lifecycle hooks for attaching callbacks that will run when we need them to.

When we repeat similar pattern for similar problems, anybody familiar with the pattern should be able to quickly learn what the code does.

Conclusion: Code should be simple, not simplistic.

> "Vigorous writing is concise. A sentence should contain no unnecessary words, a paragraph no unnecessary sentences, for the same reason that a drawing should have no unnecessary lines and a machine no unnecessary parts. This requires not that the writer make all sentences short, or avoid all detail and treat subjects only in outline, but that every word tell." [Emphasis added.] ~ William Strunk, Jr., The Elements of Style

It's common to hear arguments that verbose and explicit code reads better, but with fluency in the language, concise syntax features are often superior to the more verbose alternatives: *concise code is simple compared to the syntax-heavy alternative.*

Code should be *simple*, not *simplistic.*

Given that concise code is:

- Less bug prone
- Easier to debug

And given that bugs:

- Are extremely expensive to fix
- Tend to cause more bugs
- Interrupt the flow of normal feature development

And given that concise code is also:

- Easier to write
- Easier to read
- Easier to maintain

It is worth investing in fluency with concise syntax, currying & composition. When we fail to do so for the sake of familiarity, we talk down to readers of our code so that they can better understand it, like an adult speaking baby-talk to a toddler.

Assume the reader knows nothing about the implementation, but do not assume that the reader is stupid, or that the reader doesn't know the language.

Be clear, but don't dumb it down. To dumb things down is both wasteful and insulting. Make the investment in practice and familiarity in order to gain a better programming vocabulary, and a more vigorous style.

> Code should be simple, not simplistic.

Mocking is a Code Smell

One of the biggest complaints I hear about TDD and unit tests is that people struggle with all of the mocking required to isolate units. Some people struggle to understand how their unit tests are even meaningful. In fact, I've seen developers get so lost in mocks, fakes, and stubs that they wrote entire files of unit tests where *no actual implementation code was exercised at all.* Oops.

On the other end of the spectrum, it's common to see developers get so sucked into the dogma of TDD that they think they absolutely must achieve 100% code coverage, *by any means necessary*, even if that means they have to make their codebase more complex to pull it off.

I frequently tell people that mocking is a code smell, but most developers pass through a stage in their TDD skills where they want to achieve 100% unit test coverage, and can't imagine a world in which they do not use mocks extensively. In order to squeeze mocks into their application, they tend to wrap dependency injection functions around their units or (worse), pack services into dependency injection containers.

Angular takes this to an extreme by baking dependency injection right into all Angular component classes, tempting users to view dependency injection as the primary means of decoupling. But dependency injection is not the best way to accomplish decoupling.

TDD should lead to better design.

> The process of learning effective TDD is the process of learning how to build more modular applications.

TDD tends to have a simplifying effect on code, not a complicating effect. If you find that your code gets harder to read or maintain when you make it more testable, or you have to bloat your code with dependency injection boilerplate, you're doing TDD wrong.

Don't waste your time wedging dependency injection into your app so you can mock the whole world. Chances are very good that it's hurting you more than it's helping. Writing more testable code should simplify your code. It should require fewer lines of code and more readable, flexible, maintainable constructions. Dependency injection has the opposite effect.

This text exists to teach you two things:

1. You can write decoupled code without dependency injection, and
2. Maximizing code coverage brings diminishing returns – the closer you get to 100% coverage, the more you have to complicate your application code to get even closer, which can subvert the important goal of reducing bugs in your application.

More complex code is often accompanied by more cluttered code. You want to produce uncluttered code for the same reasons you want to keep your house tidy:

- More clutter leads to more convenient places for bugs to hide, which leads to more bugs, and
- It's easier to find what you're looking for when there's less clutter to get lost in.

What is a code smell?

> "A **code smell** is a surface indication that usually corresponds to a deeper problem in the system." ~ Martin Fowler

A code smell does not mean that something is definitely wrong, or that something must be fixed right away. It is a rule of thumb that should alert you to a possible opportunity to improve something.

This text and its title in no way imply that all mocking is bad, or that you should never mock anything.

Additionally, different types of code need different levels (and different kinds) of mocks. Some code exists primarily to facilitate I/O, in which case, there is little to do other than test I/O, and reducing mocks might mean your unit test coverage would be close to 0.

If there is no logic in your code (just pipes and pure compositions), 0% unit test coverage might be acceptable, assuming your integration or functional test coverage is close to 100%. However, if there is logic (conditional expressions, assignments to variables, explicit function calls to units, etc...), you probably do need unit test coverage, and there may be opportunities to simplify your code and reduce mocking requirements.

What is a mock?

A **mock** is a test double that stands in for real implementation code during the unit testing process. A mock is capable of producing assertions about how it was manipulated by the test subject during the test run. If your test double produces assertions, it's a mock in the specific sense of the word.

The term "mock" is also used more generally to refer to the use of any kind of test double. For the purpose of this text, we'll use the words "mock" and "test double" interchangeably to match popular usage. All test doubles (dummies, spies, fakes, etc...) stand in for real code that the test subject is tightly coupled to, therefore, all test doubles are an indication of coupling, and there may be an opportunity to simplify the implementation and improve the quality of the code under test. At the same time, eliminating the need for mocking can radically simplify the tests themselves, because you won't have to construct the mocks.

What is a unit test?

Unit tests test individual units (modules, functions, classes) in isolation from the rest of the program.

Contrast unit tests with integration tests, which test integrations between two or more units, and functional tests, which test the application from the point of view of the user, including complete user interaction workflows from simulated UI manipulation, to data layer updates, and back to the user output (e.g., the on-screen representation of the app). Functional tests are a subset of integration tests, because they test all of the units of an application, integrated in the context of the running application.

In general, units are tested using only the public interface of the unit (aka "public API" or "surface area"). This is referred to as black box testing. Black box testing leads to less brittle tests, because the implementation details of a unit tend to change more over time than the public API of the unit. If you use white box testing, where tests are aware of implementation details, any change to the implementation details could break the test, even if the public API continues to function as expected. In other words, white-box testing leads to wasted rework.

What is test coverage?

Code coverage refers to the amount of code covered by test cases. Coverage reports can be created by instrumenting the code and recording which lines were exercised during a test run. In general, we try to produce a high level of coverage, but code coverage starts to deliver diminishing returns as it gets closer to 100%.

In my experience, increasing coverage beyond ~90% seems to have little continued correlation with lower bug density.

Why would that be? Doesn't 100% tested code mean that we know with 100% certainty that the code does what it was designed to do?

It turns out, it's not that simple.

What most people don't realize is that there are two kinds of coverage:

1. **Code coverage:** how much of the code is exercised, and
2. **Case coverage:** how many of the use-cases are covered by the test suites

Case coverage refers to use-case scenarios: How the code will behave in the context of real world environment, with real users, real networks, and even hackers intentionally trying to subvert the design of the software for nefarious purposes.

Coverage reports identify code-coverage weaknesses, not case-coverage weaknesses. The same code may apply to more than one use-case, and a single use-case may depend on code outside the subject-under-test, or even in a separate application or 3rd party API.

Because use-cases may involve the environment, multiple units, users, and networking conditions, it is impossible to cover all required use-cases with a test suite that only contains unit tests. Unit tests by definition test units in isolation, **not in integration**, meaning that a test suite containing only unit tests will always have close to 0% case coverage for **integration** and **functional** use-case scenarios.

100% code coverage does not guarantee 100% case coverage.

Developers targeting 100% code coverage are chasing the wrong metric.

What is tight coupling?

The need to mock in order to achieve unit isolation for the purpose of unit tests is caused by coupling between units. Tight coupling makes code more rigid and brittle: more likely to break when changes are required. In general, less coupling is desirable for its own sake because it makes code easier to extend and maintain. The fact that it also makes testing easier by eliminating the need for mocks is just icing on the cake.

From this we can deduce that if we're mocking something, there may be an opportunity to make our code more flexible by reducing the coupling between units. Once that's done, you won't need the mocks anymore.

Coupling is the degree to which a unit of code (module, function, class, etc...) depends upon other units of code. Tight coupling, or a high degree of coupling, refers to how likely a unit is to break when changes are made to its dependencies. In other words, the tighter the coupling, the harder it is to maintain or extend the application. Loose coupling reduces the complexity of fixing bugs and adapting the application to new use-cases.

Coupling takes different forms:

- **Subclass coupling**: Subclasses are dependent on the implementation and entire hierarchy of the parent class: the tightest form of coupling available in OO design.
- **Control dependencies**: Code that controls its dependencies by telling them what to do, e.g., passing method names, etc... If the control API of the dependency changes, the dependent code will break.
- **Mutable state dependencies**: Code that shares mutable state with other code, e.g., can change properties on a shared object. If relative timing of mutations change, it could break dependent code. If timing is nondeterministic, it may be impossible to achieve program correctness without a complete overhaul of all dependent units: e.g., there may be an irreparable tangle of race conditions. Fixing one bug could cause others to appear in other dependent units.
- **State shape dependencies**: Code that shares data structures with other code, and only uses a subset of the structure. If the shape of the shared structure changes, it could break the dependent code.
- **Event/message coupling**: Code that communicates with other units via message passing, events, etc...

What causes tight coupling?

Tight coupling has many causes:

- **Mutation** vs immutability
- **Side-Effects** vs purity/isolated side-effects
- **Responsibility overload** vs Do One Thing (DOT)
- **Procedural instructions** vs describing structure
- **Imperative composition** vs declarative composition

Imperative and object-oriented code is more susceptible to tight coupling than functional code. That doesn't mean that programming in a functional style makes your code immune to tight coupling, but functional code uses pure functions as the elemental unit of composition, and pure functions are less vulnerable to tight coupling by nature.

Pure functions:

- Given the same input, always return the same output, and
- Produce no side-effects

How do pure functions reduce coupling?

- **Immutability**: Pure functions don't mutate existing values. They return new ones, instead.
- **No side effects**: The only observable effect of a pure function is its return value, so there's no chance for it to interfere with the operation of other functions that may be observing external state such as the screen, the DOM, the console, standard out, the network, or the disk.
- **Do one thing**: Pure functions do one thing: Map some input to some corresponding output, avoiding the responsibility overload that tends to plague object and class-based code.
- **Structure, not instructions**: Pure functions can be safely memoized, meaning that, if the system had infinite memory, any pure function could be replaced with a lookup table that uses the function's input as an index to retrieve a corresponding value from the table. In other words, pure functions describe structural relationships between data, not instructions for the computer to follow, so two different sets of conflicting instructions running at the same time can't step on each other's toes and cause problems.

What does composition have to do with mocking?

Everything. The essence of all software development is the process of breaking a large problem down into smaller, independent pieces (decomposition) and composing the solutions together to form an application that solves the large problem (composition).

Mocking is required when our decomposition strategy has failed.

Mocking is required when the units used to break the large problem down into smaller parts depend on each other. Put another way, *mocking is required when our supposed atomic units of composition are not really atomic,* and our decomposition strategy has failed to decompose the larger problem into smaller, independent problems.

When decomposition succeeds, it's possible to use a generic composition utility to compose the pieces back together. Examples:

- Function composition, e.g., `lodash/fp/compose`
- Component composition e.g., composing higher-order components with function composition
- State store/model composition e.g., Redux combineReducers[67]
- Object or factory composition e.g., mixins or functional mixins
- Process composition e.g., transducers
- Promise or monadic composition e.g., `asyncPipe()`, Kleisli composition with `composeM()`, `composeK()`, etc…
- etc…

When you use generic composition utilities, each element of the composition can be unit tested in isolation *without mocking the others.*

The compositions themselves will be declarative, so they'll contain *zero unit-testable logic* (presumably the composition utility is a third party library with its own unit tests).

Under those circumstances, there's nothing meaningful to unit test. You need integration tests, instead.

Let's contrast imperative vs declarative composition using a familiar example:

```
// Function composition OR
// import pipe from 'lodash/fp/flow';
const pipe = (...fns) => x => fns.reduce((y, f) => f(y), x);

// Functions to compose
const g = n => n + 1;
const f = n => n * 2;

// Imperative composition
const doStuffBadly = x => {
  const afterG = g(x);
  const afterF = f(afterG);
  return afterF;
```

---

[67] http://redux.js.org/docs/api/combineReducers.html

```
14  };
15
16  // Declarative composition
17  const doStuffBetter = pipe(g, f);
18
19  console.log(
20    doStuffBadly(20), // 42
21    doStuffBetter(20) // 42
22  );
```

Function composition is the process of applying a function to the return value of another function. In other words, you create a pipeline of functions, then pass a value to the pipeline, and the value will go through each function like a stage in an assembly line, transforming the value in some way before it's passed to the next function in the pipeline. Eventually, the last function in the pipeline returns the final value.

```
1  initialValue -> [g] -> [f] -> result
```

It is the primary means of organizing application code in every mainstream language, regardless of paradigm. Even Java uses functions (methods) as the primary message passing mechanism between different class instances.

You can compose functions manually (imperatively), or automatically (declaratively). In languages without first-class functions, you don't have much choice. You're stuck with imperative. In JavaScript (and almost all the other major popular languages), you can do it better with declarative composition.

Imperative style means that we're commanding the computer to do something step-by-step. It's a how-to guide. In the example above, the imperative style says:

1. Take an argument and assign it to x
2. Create a binding called afterG and assign the result of g(x) to it
3. Create a binding called afterF and assign the result of f(afterG) to it
4. Return the value of afterF.

The imperative style version requires logic that should be tested. I know those are just simple assignments, but I've frequently seen (and written) bugs where I pass or return the wrong variable.

Declarative style means we're telling the computer the relationships between things. It's a description of structure using equational reasoning. The declarative example says:

- doStuffBetter *is* the piped composition of g and f.

That's it.

Assuming f and g have their own unit tests, and pipe() has its own unit tests (use flow() from Lodash or pipe() from Ramda, and it will), there's no new logic here to unit test.

In order for this style to work correctly, the units we compose need to be *decoupled.*

How do we remove coupling?

To remove coupling, we first need a better understanding of where coupling dependencies come from. Here are the main sources, roughly in order of how tight the coupling is:

Tight coupling:

- Class inheritance (coupling is multiplied by each layer of inheritance and each descendant class)
- Global variables
- Other mutable global state (browser DOM, shared storage, network, etc...)
- Module imports with side-effects
- Implicit dependencies from compositions, e.g., `const enhancedWidgetFactory = compose(eventEmitter, widgetFactory, enhancements);` where `widgetFactory` depends on `eventEmitter`
- Dependency injection containers
- Dependency injection parameters
- Control parameters (an outside unit is controlling the subject unit by telling it what to do)
- Mutable parameters

Loose coupling:

- Module imports without side-effects (in black box testing, not all imports need isolating)
- Message passing/pubsub
- Immutable parameters (can still cause shared dependencies on state shape)

Ironically, most of the sources of coupling are mechanisms originally designed to reduce coupling. That makes sense, because in order to recompose our smaller problem solutions into a complete application, they need to integrate and communicate somehow. There are good ways, and bad ways. The sources that cause tight coupling should be avoided whenever it's practical to do so. The loose coupling options are generally desirable in a healthy application.

You might be confused that I classified dependency injection containers and dependency injection parameters in the "tight coupling" group, when so many books and blog post categorize them as "loose coupling".

I draw the line with a simple litmus test:

Can the unit be tested without mocking dependencies? If it can't, it's *tightly coupled* to the mocked dependencies.

The more dependencies your unit has, the more likely it is that there may be problematic coupling. Now that we understand how coupling happens, what can we do about it?

1. **Use pure functions** as the atomic unit of composition, as opposed to classes, imperative procedures, or mutating functions.

2. **Isolate side-effects** from the rest of your program logic. That means don't mix logic with I/O (including network I/O, rendering UI, logging, etc...).
3. **Remove dependent logic** from imperative compositions so that they can become declarative compositions which don't need their own unit tests. If there's no logic, there's nothing meaningful to unit test.

That means that the code you use to set up network requests and request handlers won't need unit tests. Use integration tests for those, instead.

That bears repeating:

> Don't unit test I/O. I/O is for integrations. Use integration tests, instead.

It's perfectly OK to mock and fake for integration tests.

Use pure functions

Using pure functions takes a little practice, and without that practice, it's not always clear how to write a pure function to do what you want to do. Pure functions can't directly mutate global variables, the arguments passed into them, the network, the disk, or the screen. All they can do is return a value.

If you're passed an array or an object, and you want to return a changed version of that object, you can't just make the changes to the object and return it. You have to create a new copy of the object with the required changes. You can do that with the array accessor methods[68], `Object.assign()`, or the array or object spread syntax. For example:

```
// Not pure
const signInUser = user => user.isSignedIn = true;

const foo = {
  name: 'Foo',
  isSignedIn: false
};

// Foo is mutated
console.log(
  signInUser(foo), // true
  foo              // { name: "Foo", isSignedIn: true }
);
```

vs...

---
[68]https://developer.mozilla.org/en-US/docs/Web/JavaScript/Reference/Global_Objects/Array/prototype

```javascript
// Pure
const signInUser = user => ({...user, isSignedIn: true });

const foo = {
  name: 'Foo',
  isSignedIn: false
};

// Foo is not mutated
console.log(
  signInUser(foo), // { name: "Foo", isSignedIn: true }
  foo              // { name: "Foo", isSignedIn: false }
);
```

Alternatively, you can try a library for immutable data types, such as Mori[69] or Immutable.js[70]. I'm hopeful that we'll someday get a nice set of immutable datatypes similar to Clojure's in JavaScript, but I'm not holding my breath.

You may think that returning new objects could cause a performance hit because we're creating a new object instead of reusing the existing ones, but a fortunate side-effect of that is that we can detect changes to objects by using an identity comparison (=== check), so we don't have to traverse through the entire object to discover if anything has changed.

You can use that trick to make React components render faster if you have a complex state tree that you may not need to traverse in depth with each render pass. Inherit from `PureComponent` and it implements `shouldComponentUpdate()` with a shallow prop and state comparison. When it detects identity equality, it knows that nothing has changed in that part of the state tree and it can move on without a deep state traversal.

Pure functions can also be memoized, meaning that you don't have to build the whole object again if you've seen the same inputs before. You can trade computation complexity for memory and store pre-calculated values in a lookup table. For computationally expensive processes which don't require unbounded memory, this may be a great optimization strategy.

Another property of pure functions is that, because they have no side-effects, it's safe to distribute complex computations over large clusters of processors, using a divide-and-conquer strategy. This tactic is often employed to process images, videos, or audio frames using massively parallel GPUs originally designed for graphics, but now commonly used for lots of other purposes, like scientific computing.

In other words, mutation isn't always faster, and it is often orders of magnitude slower because it prevents these kinds of macro-optimizations.

---

[69] http://swannodette.github.io/mori/
[70] https://facebook.github.io/immutable-js/

Isolate side-effects from the rest of your program logic

There are several strategies that can help you isolate side-effects from the rest of your program logic. Here are some of them:

1. **Use pub/sub** to decouple I/O from views and program logic. Rather than directly triggering side-effects in UI views or program logic, emit an event or action object describing an event or intent.
2. **Isolate logic from I/O** e.g., compose functions which return promises using `asyncPipe()`.
3. **Use objects that represent future computations** rather than directly triggering computation with I/O, e.g., `call()` from redux-saga[71] doesn't actually call a function. Instead, it returns an object with a reference to a function and its arguments, and the saga middleware calls it for you. That makes `call()` and all the functions that use it *pure functions*, which are easy to unit test with *no mocking required.*

Use pub/sub

Pub/sub is short for the publish/subscribe pattern. In the publish/subscribe pattern, units don't directly call each other. Instead, they publish messages that other units (subscribers) can listen to. Publishers don't know what (if any) units will subscribe, and subscribers don't know what (if any) publishers will publish.

Pub/sub is baked into the Document Object Model (DOM). Any component in your application can listen to events dispatched from DOM elements, such as mouse movements, clicks, scroll events, keystrokes, and so on. Back when everyone built web apps with jQuery, it was common to jQuery custom events to turn the DOM into a pub/sub event bus to decouple view rendering concerns from state logic.

Pub/sub is also baked into Redux. In Redux, you create a global model for application state (called the store). Instead of directly manipulating models, views and I/O handlers dispatch action objects to the store. An action object has a special key, called `type` which various reducers can listen for and respond to. Additionally, Redux supports middleware, which can also listen for and respond to specific action types. This way, your views don't need to know anything about how your application state is handled, and the state logic doesn't need to know anything about the views.

It also makes it trivial to patch into the dispatcher via middleware and trigger cross-cutting concerns, such as action logging/analytics, syncing state with storage or the server, and patching in realtime communication features with servers and network peers.

Isolate logic from I/O

Sometimes you can use monad compositions (like promises) to eliminate dependent logic from your compositions. For example, the following function contains logic that you can't unit test without mocking all of the async functions:

---

[71]https://github.com/redux-saga/redux-saga

```javascript
async function uploadFiles({user, folder, files}) {
  const dbUser = await readUser(user);
  const folderInfo = await getFolderInfo(folder);
  if (await haveWriteAccess({dbUser, folderInfo})) {
    return uploadToFolder({dbUser, folderInfo, files });
  } else {
    throw new Error("No write access to that folder");
  }
}
```

Let's throw in some helper pseudo-code to make it runnable:

```javascript
const log = (...args) => console.log(...args);

// Ignore these. In your real code you'd import
// the real things.
const readUser = () => Promise.resolve(true);
const getFolderInfo = () => Promise.resolve(true);
const haveWriteAccess = () => Promise.resolve(true);
const uploadToFolder = () => Promise.resolve('Success!');

// gibberish starting variables
const user = '123';
const folder = '456';
const files = ['a', 'b', 'c'];

async function uploadFiles({user, folder, files}) {
  const dbUser = await readUser({ user });
  const folderInfo = await getFolderInfo({ folder });
  if (await haveWriteAccess({dbUser, folderInfo})) {
    return uploadToFolder({dbUser, folderInfo, files });
  } else {
    throw new Error("No write access to that folder");
  }
}

uploadFiles({user, folder, files})
  .then(log)
;
```

And now refactor it to use promise composition via `asyncPipe()`:

```
1  const asyncPipe = (...fns) => x => (
2    fns.reduce(async (y, f) => f(await y), x)
3  );
4
5  const uploadFiles = asyncPipe(
6    readUser,
7    getFolderInfo,
8    haveWriteAccess,
9    uploadToFolder
10 );
11
12 uploadFiles({user, folder, files})
13   .then(log)
14 ;
```

The conditional logic is easily removed because promises have conditional branching built-in. The idea is that logic and I/O don't mix well, so we want to remove the logic from the I/O dependent code.

In order to make this kind of composition work, we need to ensure 2 things:

1. `haveWriteAccess()` will reject if the user doesn't have write access. That moves the conditional logic into the promise context so we don't have to unit test it or worry about it at all (promises have their own tests baked into the JS engine code).
2. Each of these functions takes and resolves with the same data type. We could create a `pipelineData` type for this composition which is just an object containing the following keys: `{ user, folder, files, dbUser?, folderInfo? }`. This creates a structure sharing dependency between the components, but you can use more generic versions of these functions in other places and specialize them for this pipeline with thin wrapping functions.

With those conditions met, it's trivial to test each of these functions in isolation from each other without mocking the other functions. Since we've extracted all of the logic out of the pipeline, there's nothing meaningful left to unit test in this file. All that's left to test are the integrations.

> Remember: Logic and I/O are separate concerns. Logic is thinking. Effects are actions. Think before you act!

Use objects that represent future computations

The strategy used by redux-saga is to use objects that represent future computations. The idea is similar to returning a monad, except that it doesn't always have to be a monad that gets returned. Monads are capable of composing functions with the chain operation, but you can manually chain functions using imperative-style code, instead. Here's a rough sketch of how redux-saga does it:

```javascript
// sugar for console.log we'll use later
const log = msg => console.log(msg);


const call = (fn, ...args) => ({ fn, args });
const put = (msg) => ({ msg });


// imported from I/O API
const sendMessage = msg => Promise.resolve('some response');


// imported from state handler/Reducer
const handleResponse = response => ({
  type: 'RECEIVED_RESPONSE',
  payload: response
});

const handleError = err => ({
  type: 'IO_ERROR',
  payload: err
});


function* sendMessageSaga (msg) {
  try {
    const response = yield call(sendMessage, msg);
    yield put(handleResponse(response));
  } catch (err) {
    yield put(handleError(err));
  }
}
```

You can see all the calls being made in your unit tests without mocking the network API or invoking any side-effects. Bonus: This makes your application extremely easy to debug without worrying about nondeterministic network state, etc...

Want to simulate what happens in your app when a network error occurs? Easy:

```javascript
iter.throw(NetworkError)
```

Elsewhere, some library middleware is driving the function, and actually triggering the side-effects in the production application:

```
const iter = sendMessageSaga('Hello, world!');

// Returns an object representing the status and value:
const step1 = iter.next();

log(step1);
/* =>
{
  done: false,
  value: {
    fn: sendMessage
    args: ["Hello, world!"]
  }
}
*/
```

Destructure the `call()` object from the yielded value to inspect or invoke the future computation:

```
const { value: {fn, args }} = step1;
```

Effects run in the real middleware. You can skip this part when you're testing and debugging:

```
const step2 = fn(args);

step2.then(log); // "some response"
```

If you want to simulate a network response without mocking APIs or the http calls, you can pass a simulated response into .next():

```
iter.next(simulatedNetworkResponse);
```

From there you can keep calling `.next()` until `done` is `true`, and your function is finished running.

Using generators and representations of computations in your unit tests, you can simulate everything *up to but excluding* invoking the real side-effects. You can pass values into `.next()` calls to fake responses, or throw errors at the iterator to fake errors and promise rejections.

Using this style, there's no need to mock anything in unit tests, even for complex integrational workflows with lots of side-effects.

"Code smells" are warning signs, not laws. Mocks are not evil.

All this stuff about using better architecture is great, but in the real world, we have to use other people's APIs, and integrate with legacy code, and there are lots of APIs that aren't pure. Isolated test doubles may be useful in those cases. For example, express passes shared mutable state and models side-effects via continuation passing.

Let's look at a common example. People try to tell me that express apps need dependency injection because how else will you unit test all the stuff that goes into the express app? E.g.:

```
const express = require('express');
const app = express();

app.get('/', function (req, res) {
  res.send('Hello World!')
});

app.listen(3000, function () {
  console.log('Example app listening on port 3000!')
});
```

In order to "unit test" *this file*, we'd have to work up a dependency injection solution and then pass mocks for everything into it (possibly including `express()` itself). If this was a very complex file where different request handlers were using different features of express, and counting on that logic to be there, you'd probably have to come up with a pretty sophisticated fake to make that work. I've seen developers create elaborate fakes and mocks of things like express, the session middleware, log handlers, realtime network protocols, you name it. I've faced hard mocking questions myself, but the correct answer is simple.

This file doesn't need unit tests.

The server definition file for an express app is by definition the app's main **integration** point. Testing an express handler is by definition testing an integration between your program logic, express, and all the handlers for that express app. You absolutely should not skip integration tests even if you can achieve 100% unit test coverage.

Instead of trying to unit test this file, isolate your program logic into separate units, and unit test those files. Write real integration tests for the server file, meaning you'll actually hit the network, or at least create the actual http messages, complete with headers using a tool like supertest[72].

Let's refactor the Hello World express example to make it more testable:

---

[72]https://github.com/visionmedia/supertest

Pull the `hello` handler into its own file and write unit tests for it. No need to mock the rest of the app components. This obviously isn't a pure function, so we'll need to spy on the response object to make sure we call `.send()`.

```
1  const hello = (req, res) => res.send('Hello World!');
```

You could test it something like this. Swap out the `if` statement for your favorite test framework expectation:

```
1  {
2    const expected = 'Hello World!';
3    const msg = `should call .send() with ${ expected }`;
4
5    const res = {
6      send: (actual) => {
7        if (actual !== expected) {
8          throw new Error(`NOT OK ${ msg }`);
9        }
10       console.log(`OK: ${ msg }`);
11     }
12   }
13
14   hello({}, res);
15 }
```

Pull the listen handler into its own file and write unit tests for it, too. We have the same problem here. Express handlers are not pure, so we need to spy on the logger to make sure it gets called. Testing is similar to the previous example:

```
1  const handleListen = (log, port) => () => log(`Example app listening on port ${ port\
2  }!`);
```

All that's left in the server file now is integration logic:

```
1  const express = require('express');
2
3  const hello = require('./hello.js');
4  const handleListen = require('./handleListen');
5  const log = require('./log');
6
7  const port = 3000;
8  const app = express();
9
10 app.get('/', hello);
11
12 app.listen(port, handleListen(port, log));
```

You still need integration tests for this file, but further unit tests won't meaningfully enhance your case coverage. There is certainly no need for any dependency injection framework for express apps.

Mocking is great for integration tests

Because integration tests test collaborative integrations between units, it's perfectly OK to fake servers, network protocols, network messages, and so on in order to reproduce all the various conditions you'll encounter during communication with other units, potentially distributed across clusters of CPUs or separate machines on a network.

Sometimes you'll want to test how your unit will communicate with a 3rd party API, and sometimes those API's are prohibitively expensive to test for real. You can record real workflow transactions against the real services and replay them from a fake server to test how well your unit integrates with a third party service actually running in a separate network process. Often this is the best way to test things like "did we see the correct message headers?"

There are lots of useful integration testing tools that throttle network bandwidth, introduce network lag, produce network errors, and otherwise test lots of other conditions that are impossible to test using unit tests which mock away the communication layer.

It's impossible to achieve 100% case coverage without integration tests. Don't skip them even if you manage to achieve 100% unit test coverage. Sometimes 100% is not 100%.

Made in the USA
Coppell, TX
26 January 2020